"*From Cairo to Christ* explores convert to Christ. Author Abu Atallah is an Egyptian who writes as an insider who became a believer decades ago. Those unacquainted with Islamic beliefs and practices will appreciate this easy-to-read primer."
Phil Parshall, SIM USA, author of *The Cross and the Crescent*

"This book offers a uniquely personal account of the complex and challenging journey of many who convert from Islam to Christianity. The story of Abu 'Stephen' Atallah—told with the help of his friend and coauthor Kent Van Til—is especially timely as the West struggles to meet the needs of massive numbers of Arab refugees fleeing chaos and civil war in their home countries. The authors see this humanitarian crisis as an opportunity for Christians to share the love of Christ."
John C. Knapp, president and professor, Hope College

"Abu Atallah is the real thing. I know because I am his colleague in the greatest rescue operation of our day: introducing 1.7 billion Muslims to the Savior. He could easily obtain an enviable position as a senior pastor in an American church, but like very few other Muslim-background believers, he and his dear wife have given themselves day and night to rescuing those who would like to assassinate him. This very humble, grateful account of his story is so real it's difficult to put down."
Greg Livingstone, founder, Frontiers, senior associate, World Outreach of the Evangelical Presbyterian Church

"Your heart will be stirred as Abu recounts the journey that he has been on, both prior to knowing Jesus personally and then as a fully devoted follower of Christ. His life and testimony have richly blessed my own walk with Christ. This book will cause you to consider your own commitment to the cause of Christ."
Dave Gibson, pastor of missions and evangelism, Grace Church, Eden Prairie, Minnesota

"This book is a must-read for anyone involved with Muslims and Muslim-background believers in the United States or overseas. The authors speak authentically, honesty, and truthfully. Through their words, you'll come to a deeper understanding of the culture and religious perspectives of Arab Muslims and the heart-level experiences of individuals as their faith journeys intersect with Christ and with our Western, secular, and Christian cultures."
Kate McCord, author of *In the Land of Blue Burqas*

"With enthusiasm I recommend this welcome narrative of the life of a friend who has made a journey of faith from following a prophet to embracing a faith different from the one he inherited. Academics, theologians, students, and church laity will all benefit from understanding the inside challenge of what it means to 'transfer your primary citizenship' from your own cultural context to a new commitment that reflects Matthew 6:33: 'Seek ye first the kingdom of God, and his righteousness' (KJV)."

Ray Tallman, OC International

"*From Cairo to Christ* is both a compelling first-person narrative of one Egyptian Muslim's journey to Christ and into fruitful Christian ministry among Muslims globally and also a helpful analysis of Islam and Muslims in our twenty-first-century world. Abu Atallah doesn't downplay profoundly disturbing aspects of Islam, nor does he hesitate in critiquing some embarrassing negative Christian attitudes toward Muslims. Atallah's often painful journey helpfully illuminates typical experiences for believers out of Islam as they seek to live their lives in faithfulness to their new Lord in Muslim communities, both in the Muslim world and here in the West. This short book provides invaluable perspective into the experience of those who follow Christ out of Islam as well as penetrating insights into the beliefs and experiences of Muslims in the Arab world and America today. I warmly commend it to those who desire to better understand and befriend both their Muslim neighbor and their Christian friend who was once a Muslim."

Don Little, missiologist, Pioneers, director, The Lilias Trotter Center, author of *Effective Discipling in Muslim Communities*

"*From Cairo to Christ* takes the reader through an insightful, informative, and provocative journey exploring the on-the-ground realities of the Muslim faith from the perspective of a Muslim convert to Christianity. The challenges encountered and dealt with by Abu Atallah provide fresh insights into understanding how Christians can better relate to Muslims today, in our context of religious pluralism. This book also serves as a mirror for Western Christians to more carefully critique their own understanding and practices of Christianity."

Craig Van Gelder, emeritus professor of congregational mission, Luther Seminary

From
CAIRO
to
CHRIST

HOW ONE MUSLIM'S FAITH JOURNEY

SHOWS THE WAY FOR OTHERS

ABU ATALLAH
KENT A. VAN TIL

IVP Books

An imprint of InterVarsity Press
Downers Grove, Illinois

InterVarsity Press
P.O. Box 1400, Downers Grove, IL 60515-1426
ivpress.com
email@ivpress.com

InterVarsity Press® is the book-publishing division of InterVarsity Christian Fellowship/USA®, a movement of students and faculty active on campus at hundreds of universities, colleges, and schools of nursing in the United States of America, and a member movement of the International Fellowship of Evangelical Students. For information about local and regional activities, visit intervarsity.org.

All Scripture quotations, unless otherwise indicated, are taken from THE HOLY BIBLE, NEW INTERNATIONAL VERSION®, NIV® Copyright © 1973, 1978, 1984, 2011 by Biblica, Inc.™ Used by permission. All rights reserved worldwide.

While any stories in this book are true, some names and identifying information may have been changed to protect the privacy of individuals.

Cover design: Cindy Kiple
Interior design: Daniel van Loon
Images: Egyptian man: Cultura RM Exclusive/Seb Oliver/Getty Images
         Muslim man: © Henk Badenhorst/iStockphoto

ISBN 978-0-8308-4509-5 (print)
ISBN 978-0-8308-9083-5 (digital)

Printed in the United States of America ∞

Library of Congress Cataloging-in-Publication Data
Names: Atallah, Abu, author.
Title: From Cairo to Christ : how one Muslim's faith journey shows the way
   for others / Abu Atallah and Kent A. Van Til.
Description: Downers Grove : InterVarsity Press, 2017. | Includes
   bibliographical references and index.
Identifiers: LCCN 2017017972 (print) | LCCN 2017010175 (ebook) | ISBN
   9780830890835 (eBook) | ISBN 9780830845095 (pbk. : alk. paper)
Subjects: LCSH: Atallah, Abu. | Christian converts from Islam--Biography. |
   Missions to Muslims.
Classification: LCC BV2626.4.A83 (print) | LCC BV2626.4.A83 A3 2017 (ebook) |
   DDC 248.2/467092 [B] --dc23
LC record available at https://lccn.loc.gov/2017017972

| P | 21 | 20 | 19 | 18 | 17 | 16 | 15 | 14 | 13 | 12 | 11 | 10 | 9 | 8 | 7 | 6 | 5 | 4 | 3 | 2 | 1 |
| Y | 34 | 33 | 32 | 31 | 30 | 29 | 28 | 27 | 26 | 25 | 24 | 23 | 22 | 21 | 20 | 19 | 18 | 17 |

Abu (Stephen): I dedicate this book to my wife, Belinda,
and my two children, Nathaniel and Rebecca,
who had to sacrifice seeing their father
so that he could serve the kingdom of God.
Thank you for letting me serve the Lord. I love you.
And to my fellow BMBs (believers of Muslim background)
in the Arab World for enriching my life with all their stories
and allowing me to be a part of their lives.

Kent: I would like to dedicate this book to the missionaries,
including Stephen, who have made so many sacrifices for Christ.

CONTENTS

PROLOGUE

Kent A. Van Til

In the past forty years, more Muslims have converted to Christianity than did during the previous fourteen hundred years." So said Abu Atallah in 2014. And if anyone is able to make such a statement, it is Abu. He is a convert from Islam to Christianity himself, and has been instrumental in bringing hundreds of those Muslims to Christ through his own ministry.

I know Abu under his English name, Stephen. We met while we were both seminary students in the 1980s. I didn't know him all that well at the time, though I remember well his humor and some of his hardships. I moved on to missions in Latin America and then to academics, and lost track of him. When we had a "chance" reunion a few years back, I naturally asked what he had been up to. He told me. And the more he told me, the more amazed I became. I was convinced that someone had to get this story out. Shortly thereafter I realized that I was the one that had to do it. So what follows is Stephen's story, through my words and in his voice.

Born into a well-to-do family in Cairo in the late 1950s, Stephen was a popular and outgoing Egyptian kid. He suffered the deaths of two close relatives early in life, and began asking fundamental religious questions at an early age. He sought companionship and solace in the Muslim Brotherhood, but found only violence there and quickly left.

The love of Christ found Stephen. He saw it in other Christian students, but most importantly in Christ himself. His conversion was costly. He lost family, friends, career, and home. He slept on floors and was effectively kicked out of college. His life was at risk. In fact, he chose the English name Stephen due to his belief that he too would soon be martyred.

By God's grace he was able to leave Egypt and study in the United States. After earning three university-level degrees, he has dedicated his life to serving other Muslims, both those who have and who have not yet accepted Christ.

Stephen founded a church in the predominantly Arab-populated city of Dearborn, Michigan, and then moved on to be a consultant on Islam for a major mission agency based in London. He currently is a missionary for the Evangelical Presbyterian Church in Europe, working among the millions of Syrian refugees in that continent. He also runs a training and retreat center in Spain, and lectures throughout the globe.

All along the way Stephen has been a witness to the One who first loved him. He does so in personal conversations with the highest and lowest in Muslim society, and also online on various websites. He is a well-regarded evangelist on four continents.

His story is not one of pure glory or success. He has not been able to return to Egypt under his real name, for fear that he will be killed as an apostate. His own family is bicultural and has had to move often, sometimes from country to country. He usually lives at the frontier between solvency and insolvency. But when asked whether he regrets having given up so much, he is quick to respond: "I would gladly do it again for the One who has done so much for me."

I invite you to meet my friend Stephen in these pages.

CHAPTER ONE

A
KID
in
CAIRO

My father waited in line for one fish and three small loaves. When he got them, his allotment card was stamped for that day. It was all the rations he would get for his family of five each day during the war in the Suez.

We were in Port Sai'd, Egypt, late in 1956. Egyptian President Nasser had nationalized the Suez Canal earlier that year. But the British, along with the French and the Israelis, wanted to maintain control of it. So the British bombed half of the city to the ground. The area my parents lived in was safe enough, though, since the Italian consulate was just across the street, and the Italians were allied with the British. The fighting continued until pressure from the Soviet Union and the United States finally drove out the French, British, and Israelis on December 23 of that year.

We Egyptians had stereotypes about the British and French soldiers. The British soldiers were seen as awkward but kind fellows who would give Egyptian kids chocolate bars, while French soldiers were seen as haughty and elegant men who would chase Egyptian women. My mother apparently believed these stereotypes. One day, one of her friends told her that because she was light-skinned and attractive, there were some French men coming after her. She took that quite seriously. As a good Muslim woman, she was fearful for her purity and her reputation, so she fled home barefoot, leaving her sandals in the dirt with her friends.

Three weeks after the last British soldiers were expelled from Egypt, my parents had their fourth child—me. I was born six years after my next older brother, Moustafa, eight years after my eldest brother, Yasser, and ten years after my sister, Azieza. I was very much the baby of the family. In Egypt we have a saying: "The lowest grape of the bunch is the sweetest," which means that the youngest one in the family is the sweetest. I like to think that was true. I've never been a rough character, and seem to have inherited my mother's pleasant temperament.

I'm told that my sister, Azieza, was often my babysitter. I'm sure she did a good job, because fifty years later she claims that I still owe her for all her labors on my behalf: changing my diapers, feeding me, and so on. Yasser, my eldest brother, and I were quite close. He was in school ahead of me and paved the way for all of us by being a very good student. Moustafa was close to me too, though he is a rather private person.

My father was a teacher. He had a master's degree in the fine arts, with a specialization in pottery making. He was very artistic, and I still have some pencil sketches he made of Charlie Chaplin, Laurel and Hardy, and Clark Gable and Vivien Leigh. He much admired the art of Vincent van Gogh and kept prints of van Gogh paintings around the house. Most of the males in his family, though, were engineers. His father, the grandfather I never knew, was a relatively wealthy man. He took two wives and many more mistresses. He was of Turkish origin (as are many in Egypt, which had once been part of the Ottoman Empire). He was even called a "pasha," a royal title that enabled him to be a part of the House of Lords. I still have a picture of him in a fine suit, wearing a Turkish-style fez, with gold chains, and a gold pocket watch. He spent most of his money on women singers and dancers, but he did manage to help his four sons get a good education.

My uncle Sai'id was sent by the Egyptian Ministry of Education to get a PhD in architecture at the Sorbonne in France. He sent half the money from his scholarship back home to his mother, so she would have enough to take care of his younger brothers. Uncle Sai'id later became dean of the faculty of arts in Egypt. Another uncle, Mustafa, was blind; he died at the age of thirty-six, so I never knew him. They called him "Sheik Mustafa." He was capable of reciting the entire Qur'an from memory in its original Arabic. My father's third brother, Sabri, was the black sheep of the family. He was usually drunk, and sometimes stole money from family members. My dad and Uncle Sai'id were ashamed of him and yet felt responsible for him. My mother always felt sorry for him too, and gave him a good meal and some pocket change every time he dropped in.

My father had such a fine education that he was able to work his way up in the Egyptian education department, and moved around to take advantage of the promotions. As a result, each of us children was born in a different city. Shortly after the war in the Suez was over, we moved to a more upscale Cairo suburb, where he worked as a school administrator. As a tot, I would jump up in my father's arms when he came home from work, hug him, and ask for a mint. He always gave me the mint, as well as a little nip or bite on the cheek, which is a common Egyptian way of showing affection.

When I was only six, my father took a position in Libya at the request of the Libyan government. At that time Egypt had far more professionals than any other country in North Africa, so it made agreements with other nations who needed our help. The king of Libya (Sanusi) requested that Egypt send professionals such as my father to teach in Libya. When he came home from Libya on school holidays, he often brought us gifts: one of them was the red tricycle that I had longed for. He also took me out for my favorite dessert, caramelized bread. It's no wonder that by the time I was twenty I had seven fillings in my teeth. Of course, the fact that I also stole sugar cubes from the kitchen might have contributed to this. Like most Egyptians, I have a sweet tooth.

My father's high position in the education department of Nasser's regime enabled him to earn far more money than most Egyptians. In Libya his title was the Assistant to the Secretary of Education. Given Libya's oil revenues, he must have been paid very well, and like my grandpa, the pasha, he liked to spend his money. He wore expensive English summer-wool suits, and he bought one for me too. It had eleven pockets! (I counted.) He once came home from Libya with a new Mercedes. My mother, however, was wiser, and she immediately made him sell it, and then used the money to buy property on which they could build a house.

My father was not an especially religious man. He went to the mosque to pray on Fridays, but wasn't very active throughout the week. He believed that his good intentions and deeds would probably be enough to get him into paradise. In Islam you get credit for good intentions as well as good deeds. And you also get credit for not doing wrong. So at the Last Judgment you have a good chance of getting into paradise if you did relatively little wrong and intended to do considerable good. The angel on your right will hold a book listing your good deeds, and the angel on the left, your evil deeds. The books are then placed on a scale. If the good deeds outweigh the evil ones, you go to paradise; if the evil outweigh the good, hell.

I was a good Muslim kid myself. I obeyed the call of the *muezzin* from the minaret, who called the faithful to prayer five times a day.[1]

I testify that there is no God but Allah.
I testify that Mohammed is God's Prophet.
Come to prayer.
Come to security [or salvation].
God is the greatest.
There is no God but Allah.

Since my maternal grandmother was also of Turkish descent, she too was lighter skinned than most Egyptians, which is considered a great advantage. In fact, in Egypt and through much of the Arab-speaking world, blacks are still unofficially referred to as slaves and considered inferior. So my mother pushed me and my siblings to stay away from dark-skinned Egyptians. As it turns out, she got her wish: we all married blondes.

My mother lost her own mother when she was only seven. She had a two-year-old sister, who she took care of while doing the household chores. She learned responsibility the hard way, at an early age. My maternal grandfather later remarried and had a son.

That boy grew very close to my mother and remains a dear uncle to me. Mother was also more religious than my father was: she has prayed five times a day to Allah ever since she was seven years old, just as the Qur'an dictates.

The home my mother bought (my father was working in Libya) eventually became a four-story complex that was intended to house each of us as we got married and raised our own families. We lived on the third story. I know what it looks like from a number of angles, because my brothers Yasser and Moustafa used to dangle me by my toes from the third-floor balcony. It was a beautiful home in a district that included many embassies and foreign nationals. Since we were only blocks from the Nile, cranes, herons, and cormorants constantly plied the nearby skies. Birch and palm trees lined the streets. Each morning a Bedouin woman came in from the countryside, her donkey loaded with jugs of healthy, water-buffalo milk for sale.

My brothers and I played games, and they often made me play on a "team" against them. So there I would be at age five or six, with a rubber band and paper wads in my hands, with my two expert-marksmen elder brothers firing at me. I lost. Our district was on the outskirts of Cairo, with fields and farms nearby. We had a field to play soccer in, and the streets were completely safe. Today the neighborhood has been swallowed up by Cairo, an ever-expanding city of over eight million inhabitants.

We were even well-to-do enough to have a country-club membership. The elites of Egypt plus some British and German expats were members there. It had a pool, a movie theater, polo grounds, and so forth. We went there often, gawked at the European sunbathers, and watched Hollywood films. The club membership enabled us to flaunt our high status in society. There is an old Egyptian proverb that goes: "Eat whatever you like to eat at home, but dress the way other people think you should outside." That's what we did. We looked good in public—and were proud of it.

My grandmother also lived nearby. She was a sweet, old woman. She was blind and wanted company, so she paid me a quarter to sit still long enough for her to tell stories about the *Arabian Nights* or other parables and fables. I well remember these stories and still use some of them when I speak in public.

At that time a young *imam* (religious leader) roved around our neighborhood in a cheap cotton robe and flip-flops trying to start a new mosque in our area. Along with other local children, I went out and collected money to build the new mosque. We succeeded. Today that imam wears a silk robe and presides over a big mosque.

Family visits were quite common and rarely planned in advance. I remember one occasion when my mother had to leave for a week to help one of her family members. She carefully prepared exactly enough food for us kids while she was gone, estimating how much we would need for each meal. A few days later, relatives from my father's side of the family dropped in—all twelve of them. We greeted them and treated them like royalty, as is customary. We had to make emergency runs to the grocery store to get enough to make it through, and we had barely enough money to do it. But we did enjoy having them over, and when they departed, we told them what a pleasure it was and that they should return soon.

Bringing honor to the family is crucial in Arab societies. If I was being introduced to someone new, I would be placed in a branch of the family tree until everyone could make a connection and see where I fit in. "Oh, so your mother is the sister of X who married the son of Y. And he was the man from family T who was known to have endowed the mosque in S." It is something like a game of

Bingo. We keep talking and examining family lines till we can declare, "Bingo, we're family!" This goes back a long way in Arab tradition. Even today, different political parties are often derived from branches of families or sects that split off the Muslim trunk centuries ago.[2]

The main celebration of the year is Ramadan, which is celebrated with family. Ramadan is a month-long fast and is one of the five pillars of Islam. The fast goes from sunrise to sunset, and the forbidden items include not only food but also water, tobacco, sex, and so on. The reason for the fast is twofold: to grow in spiritual strength as the body weakens, and to remember the poor, who don't have much food for their everyday lives. The Islamic calendar is set up on lunar cycles, so the time for Ramadan changes over the years. When Ramadan comes up during a summer month, it can be very taxing, since the daytime heat in Cairo averages over 100 degrees Fahrenheit. Furthermore, the hours of daylight in the summer are far longer than they are in the winter.

Muslims know that they should be especially well behaved during Ramadan, since bad deeds eliminate the effectiveness of the fast. Nonetheless, one unintended consequence of the summer heat and the fast is that people get quite cranky toward the end of a long, hot day in which they've had neither food nor water. Fistfights are a common sight in Cairo on hot Ramadan afternoons.

At sunset the local mosque usually sets out food and water for the poor, with flags or balloons drawing attention to it. Some wealthy people also set out food, especially politicians who are seeking reelection. As children, we would carry beautifully ornate lanterns, *fanoos*, after sunset and sing songs of the season. At dusk, TV stations would broadcast shows that encouraged us to keep the fast and the faith. Breaking the fast at dusk was always, literally, a treat: we Egyptians love to eat our favorite foods, such as crepes filled with fruits or meats, baklava, honey, almonds, hazelnuts, dried figs, and apricots, at the end of a day of fasting. The end of the month of Ramadan is a three-day celebration called Eid al-Fitr. It is the nearest celebration Muslims have to the Christian Christmas. Our extended family always had a feast.

My father never made a pilgrimage to Mecca (the *hajj*). I don't know whether that was a cause of regret for him. It is said that the hajj makes up for thousands of sins.[3] The hajj is one of the five pillars of Islam; the other four are repeating the creed, "There is no God but Allah, and Muhammad is his prophet"; almsgiving; five daily prayers; and fasting during Ramadan. All Muslims who are able try to make the hajj at one point in their lives.

The hajj is an annual event that involves millions of Muslims. The pilgrims (*hajji*) replicate the journey of Muhammad and worship at the Kaaba, a building believed to have been constructed by Abraham and Ishmael (sura 2:127).[4] Pilgrims walk counter-clockwise around the Kaaba seven times, each time offering a prayer of praise to Allah. If possible, they kiss the black stone at its center, but if the crowds are too great, they devoutly raise their right hand in honor during each of the seven passes. Hajji also reenact Hagar's frantic search for water, and they throw stones at a wall where Shaytan (Satan) is believed to have dwelt. Muslims believe that going on the hajj erases all previous sins, so each pilgrim returns from it with a perfectly clean record.[5] But it is still no guarantee of a positive final judgment or ticket to paradise, since you can start sinning again the minute the hajj is over. The only guarantee of paradise is martyrdom in the cause of Islam.

There is a cute Algerian story about an Arab cat who went on a pilgrimage to Mecca. Upon his return, he called all his friends together, including the mice, to celebrate his pilgrimage and the resulting remission of sins. One old mouse refused to come, still not trusting the cat. All the other mice happily attended. The party went on, the music played, and the cat talked about his lovely, transformative experience on the hajj. Then he killed and ate all the mice. The old mouse who stayed home knowingly said, "A cat will still be a cat, hajj or no." The moral of the story is that even those who make the hajj cannot be confident that they will truly be changed or attain paradise.

Muslims generally believe that Ishmael, the child of Abraham and his concubine, Hagar, was the son God asked Abraham to sacrifice.[6] When the angel held back Abraham's hand to prevent the sacrifice, Abraham found a ram in the thicket and sacrificed it in Ishmael's place. In remembrance of this, the hajji celebrate with a ceremonial feast of lamb, chant praises to Allah, and give gifts to friends and family upon their return from the hajj.

One holiday, when my father was home from Libya, I saw him taking a nap. I went over to talk and play with him, but I noticed that his stomach was not rising and falling. I told my mother and brothers, but they didn't believe me. I insisted. When my mother came in, she found him dead. He had had a brain aneurism; there had been no warning. He was fifty-two years old, and I was eleven.

"Oh Baba, Baba," I cried. "How could you leave us?" I was heartbroken and have grieved over his loss ever since. At age eleven I could not comprehend why death had struck so soon. I had lost a wonderful man as father, one who had doted on me and shown me love and affection. My father's love could never be replaced, but family did step in. In Egypt, the government really has no programs for widows, so the family takes on responsibilities for one another. Uncle Sai'id, in particular, took care of us. He used the festival of Eid al-Fitr as the occasion to give our family money or new clothes.

I was a city kid, but the cousins on my mother's side lived in the country. In fact, half of one village south of Cairo on the Nile was populated with relatives on my mother's side. On one street lived an uncle in a three-story house. His adult son and family lived on the second floor, and his second son on the third. Across the street were his cousins. For dinner, all the women would get together and cook for the whole tribe. So it was—and still is—in most rural villages in Egypt.

I didn't know anything about animals or farming, but spent most summers there playing with my country cousins. We would ride the donkey together and play on the farm. I once made the mistake of standing behind a mule that was tied in his stall. He kicked me so hard I went flying to the other end of the barn. I had some badly bruised ribs. My sympathetic cousins laughed themselves to tears. "How could you be so stupid as to stand behind the mule?"

One cousin was exactly my age, and we were closer than most brothers. At harvest time we were assigned to stay up all night with the harvested crops. Since there were no barns, we had to protect the crop from thieves. So we spent the night in the field next to the cucumbers, melons, peppers, and so on. To fortify ourselves for our overnighter, we drank "tar tea," which looked a great deal like its name, since it had been brewed for over six hours. To dull the pain we added tablespoons of sugar to this black potion. I suspect the caffeine and sugar content of this concoction would make most of today's energy drinks seem watery by comparison. We lay among the vegetables, waiting for the truck that would come to pick up the produce in the morning.

My cousin and I were allowed to play throughout the whole village, most of which was made up of our relatives. But one day, when I was back in Cairo, my cousin played around the village well and fell in. He drowned at the age of eleven. I was devastated. I was at a loss to express my emotions. I had lost the two men who were closest to me in a year's time. My mother tried to console me, but my grief was a greater weight than I could bear.

My family didn't want me to attend the funeral and burial of either my cousin or my father. Perhaps they thought I was too young to be exposed to this. But because I never actually saw them buried, I was haunted by dreams for years afterward. Perhaps my father was coming home from Libya, or my cousin would soon come out to play.

Years later, when a friend of the family died, I learned what Muslim funeral practices are like. The men and the women are segregated. The wailing begins with the women, who raise their voices in loud, falling tones that would make you cry even if you didn't know the deceased. They come to the home of the widow with foodstuffs like dates and candies and try to console her. The widow will cry out often, saying something like, "Oh, dear love of mine, why did you go? What will I do without you?"

Meanwhile, the men of the family will set up a funeral tent nearby. It could be right in the middle of a street or off in the corner of a lot. They put in the tent stakes, and the male relatives sit in a circle on its edges. Other men come in and greet the relatives one by one, recalling what a good man and a good Muslim he had been. An imam with a strong voice is paid to chant from the Qur'an all night. At modern funerals, the imams use microphones, so the whole neighborhood hears the recitation. Burial must occur within twenty-four hours of death, since that is the amount of time that it took to bury the Prophet Muhammad.[7] The corpse is not embalmed. The body is wrapped in a shroud and then laid in the ground on its right side so that the good deeds will all be weighed properly.[8] The head faces Mecca in anticipation of the resurrection. After the burial, there is a three-day mourning period for all, and there is a four-month plus ten-day mourning period for the widow. During this time she is not supposed to wear any decorative clothing or jewelry, move out of her home, or remarry.

Since I was home so much with my mother after my father's death, I learned to keep house, unlike most Egyptian men. Even though my mother had gone to school through only the sixth grade, she encouraged my siblings and me to study. She read the newspaper, watched the news, and had her own independent political viewpoints, all unusual for an Egyptian woman in that day. She also kept a running list of proverbs, which she poured out on us with frequency. I still remember a few: "The baby monkey, in his mother's eye, looks like a gazelle." Or "The door of the carpenter is always jammed." I remember that she made me memorize passages from the Qur'an, a normal assignment for Muslim children. If I messed up or goofed off instead of studying, she gave me a swat with her flip-flop. She insisted that all of us go forward in our education, and we all did.

CHAPTER TWO

ADOLESCENCE
in an
ARAB FAMILY

I was a popular kid: short, talkative, outgoing, and well known in the neighborhood. I talked with everybody—the shopkeepers, the utility workers, the carpenter, the baker, and the neighbors. I made my daily rounds from one to the next. They all knew me by name, and my brothers and sister were even known as "the brother/sister of Abu." My mother complained that I blabbed family secrets all over town, and she was probably right. Sometimes I would go out and play without telling anyone where I was going, which drove my mother nuts. I was also known around the house as the "Destroyer" because I took apart anything I could get my hands on. Rarely could I put it back together. I took apart every toy I got—just to see how it worked.

I was a Boy Scout leader, and I loved my time in the club. Since the club in Egypt was founded by the British, we dressed up like the British scouts. We had scarves and hats, and worked on merit badges. I also played xylophone in the school band, while enrolled in some of the best schools of Cairo. In middle school I was a good student. In fact, I turned in the best biology notebook in the school. It was very artistic, no doubt thanks to my father's influence. I became close to some of my teachers, one student teacher in particular. He was with us for only a year, but we loved him. I still have a picture of him.

During the War of 1967, I was trained to be a civil defense worker. I had to learn what to do when we were bombarded by the Israelis in their US-made Phantom jets. I saw bodies being carried by helicopter to the nearby military hospital. To this day, when I hear a thunderstorm, I cringe, fearing that bombs may be falling.

Like most boys in Muslim countries, I was circumcised at age twelve. A party was held in my honor, somewhat like a Jewish bar mitzvah. At the party celebrating the circumcision, they sing a song called "Oh You Little Prince." It goes like this:

Oh, young little groom,
You may be hurting now,
But you won't die.
You changed clothes and dressed up
And you'll be drinking some fine chicken soup soon.

While singing this the family dances in a circle and rings a copper mortar and pestle. Unlike a bar mitzvah, however, this ritual has no real religious significance.

In high school I fell in love with a special girl. She was a beauty who, along with her sisters, had been educated in French schools and influenced by French culture. She was also my first cousin, the daughter of Uncle Sai'id. She had grown up in France while he completed his PhD at the Sorbonne. She and her sisters then attended a private French school in Egypt once they returned from Paris, and Uncle Sai'id had French paintings and decorations in his home. All this French influence made me suspicious about her past with French men. Like most Egyptian young men, I was no virgin, but I held firmly to the hypocritical belief that a woman must be a virgin on her wedding day. In spite of my doubts, I fell in love with her. To get her attention and sympathy, I made a pathetic attempt at suicide by overdosing on aspirin. I had absolutely no intention of actually dying, so I called a friend to come and get me to a hospital shortly after I took the pills. My cousin was not swayed; her rejection was heartbreaking.

Some years later, after I had become a Christian, my brother Moustafa sent me a letter explaining that I had probably become a Christian in order to salve the broken heart that was caused by my cousin's rejection. He also posited that my attraction to foreigners led to my later obsession with Christ. Perhaps those were influences, but they were certainly not the most important ones. It seems not to have occurred to Moustafa that Christianity might simply be true.

Falling in love with and marrying a cousin is commonplace in most Arab countries. Arabs want their inheritance and traditions to stay in the family, so the ideal mate is the daughter of your father's brother, which is exactly what she was. So my romantic attraction to her was applauded by my family, and they too were disappointed when I was thwarted in love. In fact, brother Yasser married her older sister, bringing great joy to the whole family.

If no cousin on your father's side is available, the next best candidate is the daughter of your mother's brother, and so on down the line. This may have its genetic problems, but in some ways it is good. The cousins have usually grown up together, and they know each other and each other's family well. This may be one reason that divorce is far less frequent among Egyptians than it is among Americans.

Yasser was a brilliant student. He went to dental school after college and then joined the military as an army dentist. He eventually became a brigadier general of the police force. It is quite common for people to get ahead in Egypt by joining the army or police. These institutions have a lot of money, and they run businesses (and hospitals) throughout the country. As the world saw in the February 2011 coup in Egypt, and the takeover in 2013, the military is highly respected—and much feared.

Yasser not only studied in Egypt but also in England, where he earned his PhD in dentistry. He is credited with a pioneering discovery in TMJ research.[1] Yet, at one point he had some emotional and physical problems. My mother tried everything she could to help him. She took him to a doctor, then to a psychologist. She lit a special candle for him in the Coptic Church,[2] and she also resorted to an Islamic folk remedy. She thought that someone might have cursed him, perhaps out of envy, so she placed an amulet under his pillow as protection. Inside the amulet was the ear of a wolf and some verses from the Qur'an. The verses were from the last two chapters of the Qur'an (chapters titled "Al-Nas" and "Al-Falaq") and are widely believed to protect successful homes and businesses from spells conjured by envious neighbors. In fact, the Prophet Muhammad himself feared that someone had put a spell on him, so he was undoubtedly relieved when the visions of "Al-Nas" and "Al-Falaq" included an antidote to such spells. These verses from the Qur'an are often hung up in Muslims homes and businesses in much the same way that Christians may have "As for me and my house, we will serve the Lord," or some such verse posted on their wall.

This is far from the only ritual practice of folk Islam. Arabic coffee is famous throughout the world for its taste. But in the Arab world it is also famous as a tool of divination. When brewed, the coffee has lots of suds. Fortunetellers take this brew, turn it over in a saucer, and read out the fortune from the suds. One man in our neighborhood was a professional fortuneteller. He would charge 500 Egyptian pounds (a small fortune) to read someone's fortune from the coffee. People would come from all over the country to have their fortunes told by him. For example, a person considering marriage would ask him to "read the cup," and see if the time and the person were auspicious. Among the general public, folk Islam runs parallel to orthodox Islam, much to the chagrin of most imams and Islamic scholars.

My sister, Azieza, earned a degree in agriculture, and she served as an agricultural consultant in dirt-poor Yemen under the auspices of the World Bank. She worked among the women there, showing them how to increase their agricultural productivity. Although women had considerable opportunities in Egypt for education and advancement, this was not true in Yemen. My sister was harassed by the Yemeni men because she helped the local women advance, which was threatening to the men who wanted to maintain complete control.

We didn't go out on dates in Egypt. It was assumed that any time spent together between eligible singles was aimed directly at marriage. In Egypt, as in most Muslim countries, a woman cannot be alone with an eligible male. So if my mother's brother came over, she and my sister could ask him into the house, and they would wear no veils or special coverings since he was not an eligible marriage candidate for either of them. If, however, any eligible man were to stop by unannounced (and that is how most visits occurred), my mother and sister would have to quickly cover up and seek a male member of the family to accompany them.

So when my sister, Azieza, went out with her fiancé, I was often sent along as her escort (spy). I was literally to be the "wedge" that stayed between them. I really didn't care whether my sister's fiancé was spending time with her, but I had to go along with the charade. Her fiancé knew we were playing a game too. So after they were together for a while, he would say to me, "Why don't you run and get us some ice cream cones? And don't go to the shop around the corner, they don't have the good stuff. Go down to Sulemain Street and get them. And buy one for yourself too. No rush." We knew it was a social game, but one that was necessary—and fun to play.

The way inheritance works in Islam is that the sons receive one full share of inheritance and the daughters get one-half share. So a common marriage would mean that the couple would receive one and a half shares from the parents. The man, however, must pay a dowry to the family of the woman. When young people marry within the family, the inheritance, which is often land, remains in that family. It is quite similar to what the Old Testament Israelites did. After my conversion, though, I lost all claim to the family inheritance since it is illegal for a Christian to receive the inheritance of a Muslim. If I were to make a claim on the inheritance today, my sisters-in-law would scream, "He apostatized! He cannot receive the inheritance of a Muslim!"

My second brother, Moustafa, became an engineer—and also a socialist. When he was an engineering student in Cairo, he joined in the protests against President Anwar Sadat and was jailed for his efforts. He likes to keep things to himself, and I am only now finding out about some of the things he did when he was younger. He is a man of principle, well read, and conscientious.

I was deeply embedded in my family, village, religion, and country. I had it made, as the youngest child in a well-to-do family. Though I lost my father at an early age, I grew up as a child of privilege in comparison to most Egyptians. I never went hungry; I had an excellent education and a loving family. I followed the customs of my faith and my culture. Therefore, it came as a great surprise to everyone, me included, when I became a Christian.

CHAPTER THREE

ENCOUNTERING
CHRIST

In my last year of high school my best friend, Abd al-Rahman,
joined the Muslim Brotherhood. The Muslim Brotherhood is a
conservative group in Egypt that believes Egypt should be an
Islamic state, complete with sharia law and a caliph.[1] His father,
Muhammad Abd al-Rahman, was the best tailor in all of Cairo,
and a fine gentleman. He had many famous clients, including
Oum Kalthoum, the most famous female singer in the Arab world
at that time. When she came to his shop, I used to hide among
the gowns to sneak a view of her. It was exciting, and gave me
something to brag about to all my friends. Many young men—and
plenty of old ones—could only dream of being in close proximity
to her.

In order to socialize with the al-Rahman family, I joined the
Muslim Brotherhood too. In doing so I not only wanted to get
close to them but also entertained the hope that Allah would
reward me with good enough grades to qualify for Cairo University.
For me, joining the Muslim Brotherhood wasn't a formal or

religiously significant event; I just took up their practices and tagged along with my friend and his father.

After he joined the Brotherhood, Muhammad Abd al-Rahman decided that he could no longer in good conscience continue his work as a tailor for women, since that kind of work required him to touch women when he measured them for their gowns. Instead he became a grocer—and ultimately a bitter and unsuccessful one. In keeping with the customs of the Brotherhood, he also forced his wife to stop using birth control and to wear a *hijab* (scarf or veil). As a result, she bore five more children over the next eight years. Muhammad began to beat his wife and children, including Abd. The entire family became poor and sullen, instead of prosperous and happy, as they had been pre-Brotherhood.

In the mid-1970s, the Muslim Brotherhood began to take very aggressive positions. They took over many labor unions, including the Student Union at Cairo University. They threatened with knifing any non-Brotherhood student who contemplated running for the Student Union. They segregated the men from the women in classes. Anyone who dared to oppose them risked death from knifing. This was too much for me. I left the Brotherhood as quickly and quietly as I had joined it.

Like my father, I wanted to pursue the fine arts. When, however, my Uncle Sai'id and brother Yasser heard of this, they tried to dissuade me, arguing that I would starve as an artist, and they were probably right. My grades were not good enough to get into medical school (like Yasser) or engineering school (like Moustafa), so I started at Cairo University as a business and accounting student. I lived at home, as did most of my fellow students, and commuted to class in a ferry that crossed the Nile River.

Since there were members of the Egyptian diplomatic corps in our neighborhood, my family had made arrangements for me to get into the civil service after college. This was a natural thing to do. If the saying "it's not what you know, it's who you know" is true in the United States, it is doubly true in the Middle East. We don't see this as immoral. In fact, it would be seen as foolish and perhaps immoral not to help out our friends and family. These relationships mean everything. So cultivating them and expecting favors in return was as important as getting good grades. I studied English as well as business, thinking it would be helpful if I were to get an international posting.

Once, while I was sitting in the cafeteria at the university, I saw one of the Muslim Brothers walk up to a young Christian woman. I knew he was one of the Muslim Brotherhood because he had a full beard, a special head covering, and he wore a shin-length robe. She was a Coptic Christian, and she wore a necklace with a cross pendant on it. He ripped the necklace off her neck, spat on her, and ground the cross pendant into the floor with his heel. He slapped her and said, "You infidel! You are going to hell!"

As you can imagine, this made quite an impression on me and the other students who were there. We were all Muslims, but in Egypt we had learned to tolerate the Copts over many centuries. After all, Egypt was once a Christian country, and Alexandria was a major Christian center before the Arabs took over. What was going on? Why were the Muslim Brothers acting this way? Some of the Muslim Brothers at the university even beat up their Christian professors, since they could not stand the idea that an infidel should rule over or teach a Muslim.[2]

There is a saying among Muslims: "Islam is perfect, though its practice is often flawed." I certainly saw the flaws in its practice when I looked at Muhammad Abd al-Rahman and the vicious Muslim Brothers at the University of Cairo.

Our neighborhood was quite cosmopolitan, and included many Europeans. One of these was the son of a German engineer who was about my age. The boy, Jansi, was an atheist like his father, who had grown up during World War II and lost all faith in God. Jansi was also a first-class womanizer. He was hot for Egyptian women, especially the Christian ones, since they were considered classier and worldlier than the plain and pure Muslim women. Some of them spoke some French or English and were known to mix socially with men. My Muslim classmates, for example, felt that it was okay to have some fun with the Christian girls before marriage, and then marry a good Muslim woman.

Jansi dragged me to a meeting where such women were to be found. To my great disappointment it turned out to be a Christian meeting in which they prayed and studied the Bible. The women there did mingle openly with men and wore no veils. They walked freely among the young men, who seemed to think it nothing unusual. *How could they!* I wondered. But there was nothing unseemly going on. The men and women treated one another as if they were brothers and sisters, not like the characters in Western soap operas, which is what I expected. I later learned that they were as surprised by my presence as I was by theirs.

One person at this meeting got up to pray, and he thanked God for helping him with his homework. *What idiocy!* I thought. Why would you expect the Lord of the universe to care about your homework? Allah is the master, and we are the slaves. Islam means "submission," so a Muslim's duty is to submit to the will of Allah, not try to influence it. The servant must please the master; the master never serves the slave. So addressing God as Father was both strange and blasphemous. How dare we bring God to our level and give him an earthly title like Father?

The prayer also seemed wrong in the very way it approached God. In Islam, prayers are clearly prescribed and programmatic. They are typically memorized chapters from the Qur'an. We know the words in advance, and we repeat the prayers five times a day, each time the muezzin calls us to prayer. We may occasionally add a few personal notes to the end of the prayer, called *Du'a'a*, but we never just pray whatever comes to mind. Reciting prayers is a good deed for which Muslims receive credit. These Christians, on the other hand, spoke to God as if they were conversing with a friend.

Allah demands submission and obedience, whereas the Christian God asks for our love. There are ninety-nine names for Allah in the Qur'an that Muslims commonly recite. One of them, *Al-Wadud*, is sometimes translated as "Loving God."[3] But a more accurate translation of *Al-Wadud* is "the Concerned or Friendly God who visits us." The actual Arabic word for love, *mahaba*, is not a name for Allah, and even *Al-Wadud* is but one of the ninety-nine names. The nature of Allah is not revealed in the Qur'an; only his will is. As a result, few Muslims will say that they know Allah himself; they only know what Allah demands. As I would soon learn, the first letter of John simply says, "God is Love." This difference between the Christian God of love and the Muslim God of law and justice would change my life. Hearing the children's song "Jesus Loves Me, This I Know" was an amazing revelation for me. God loves me? What a strange idea!

A few weeks later I had an occasion to pray in that spontaneous Christian style. My friends and I regularly held drag races in the nearby desert on Thursday nights. I was riding with a friend in his car, but we went off the trail, got stuck in the sand, and the car wouldn't start. *Okay*, I thought, *I'll try a Christian prayer. Please, Jesus, get us out of this sand pit.* Vroom! The car started up, and a truck immediately came by to pull us out. Oh well, it must have been just a coincidence. My prayer was more like that of a gambler pulling the handle on a slot machine than a prayer of faith. I just got lucky and hit the jackpot.

Some time later, at the same desert drag strip, I was riding a motorcycle my German friend had lent me. I was racing it and lost control while traveling at a high speed. I was scared of having a terrible, body-crushing accident. Whoa! Time to try that prayer technique again. *Jesus, help me!*

I quickly got the bike under control. Jansi the atheist found me and said, "God sure saved you this time."

"What do you mean?" I asked. "You're an atheist, and you're telling me it was God?" In fact, I had prayed to Jesus even though I believed that Jesus was not God, so even more doubts about God crept in.

My brother Yasser had once dated a Christian woman from Armenia while she was studying in Egypt. She had given him an Arabic Bible with the hope that he would read it and perhaps convert. But Yasser forgot about it and stuck it in a drawer. I happened (or was I predestined?) to find it there one day and began to read it sporadically. There is no way a proper Muslim should have a Bible in the house, but I was safe with this one. If someone caught me with it, I could honestly say that it wasn't mine—that I had simply found it.

From the Bible I learned a great deal. Muslims believe that the Qur'an is the divine revelation Muhammad received directly in visions, and that the Bible and the Torah are the mistaken early versions of God's revelation to Muhammad. But I began to suspect that the opposite might be the truth. When I read the Bible, I found that Jews and Christians have always prayed to their God as if conversing with a loving friend and father, and their prayers were answered. They prayed not as trembling servants to a Master but as a child to his Baba,[4] or sometimes as a sibling to an older brother—Christ. *Different*, I thought, *Very different*. I would never have thought of addressing Allah as a father or brother.

As I continued to read the Bible and observe the Christian young people I began to see a consistent message throughout. The message was that Jesus not only spoke the truth but was the truth. And the truth was that he loved us as a father and brother. He was more than a prophet. A prophet like Muhammad might have spoken the truth, but to be the truth itself required that he be more than a prophet.

I had an inkling that I might want to become a Christian, so my curiosity led me to a local Protestant church. I met with the pastor and told him I thought I would like to be baptized and become a Christian. He told me I was too young and didn't know what I was doing. He was right. So I began a two-year period of study and reflection: I read books on Christianity, met with Christians, and continued to pray to God in Christ.

To balance my growth in Christianity with my Muslim beliefs, I also bought some books in Arabic that criticized Christianity. I didn't have to look hard for them; there were dozens. According to them it would be crazy for a Muslim to convert to Christianity. Islam is perfect and true, and the Qur'an is the Word of God, revealed directly to Muhammad in visions. The Bible, on the other hand, corrupts Abraham's pure monotheism by introducing the doctrines of the Trinity and the incarnation. Its books are not one seamless series of visions like those of Muhammad, but a hodgepodge of letters, poems, histories, and so on. Christians were Crusaders and oppressors of Muslims, and Western societies were morally corrupt. Muhammad was the final prophet of God, and he alone revealed the ultimate truth of God.

The Qur'an says that all children are born naturally as good and pure Muslims, and anyone who turns from Islam to Christianity must have been corrupted by non-Muslim parents or society. Conversely, people who convert from Christianity to Islam are actually reverting back to their original condition (*fitra*).[5] I was born a Muslim, and as such was automatically a part of the community (*umma*) of God, and did not have Christian parents to corrupt me. So no one, including myself, could say why I should be attracted to Christianity. In fact, from the time of Muhammad forward, Muslims have believed that Islam should be attractive to Jews and Christians. When Muhammad received his visions, he invited the Jews and the Christians to join him, expecting their eager acceptance of his new words from God, but was surprised by their stubborn refusals.

If I were to become a Christian, it would mean not only changing my religion but changing my whole identity and bringing shame upon my family. My whole family is Muslim, and my society and culture was Muslim. My religion was not an afterthought about what life after death might be like, but a holistic understanding of what life is now. The air I breathed was Islamic. Changing from Islam to Christianity would mess up my life forever. I could not expect to get a job in the diplomatic corps or any other high-ranking position in Egypt if people found out I was Christian. Muslim women would not consider me a legitimate marriage partner. My family would disown me. I might even be considered a spy or someone who betrayed his country, his people, and his

religion. I could even lose my life—not only figuratively but literally. How could I leave country, family, and religion behind? It
was as if I would no longer exist. Becoming a Christian would be
truly crazy. Not only might I face death, I would put my family to
shame, and the worst thing that an Arab can do is to put his family
to shame.

Nonetheless, I kept having internal conflicts and continued to
raise questions. Most of them had to do with the behavior of the
Christians I was getting to know, in comparison to that of the
Muslims I had long known. There is a saying in Arabic, "Only a
rotten orange produces rotten juice." So if Christianity is so rotten,
why were the Christians I had gotten to know so good? The
Muslim Brother in the cafeteria and Abd al-Rahman's father were
far worse than the young people in the Christian group. How then
was this rotten orange of Christianity producing such good juice
while the perfect orange of Islam was producing rotten juice?

I went back to the Christian study group now and then. I continued to see the Christians relate to one another as brothers and
sisters, and to God as their own dear Baba. They kept praying and
speaking spontaneously with God. They loved their God and one
another. A Muslim like me didn't love or yearn for Allah. We
feared and obeyed Allah. The Christians turned to their God as if
he were their dearest and most beloved friend. For them it was
almost a romance; for me such a romance was a scandal.

There is no such thing as a prayer-and-share group for Muslims.
You might go to a class at the mosque and respectfully ask questions about the Qur'an, but never would you get together with
other Muslims to share your faith. Offering prayers and reciting
the Qur'an are personal duties meant to gain favor from Allah, not
to generate understanding. If you want to know what you are to do

as a Muslim, you seek a *fatwa*—an official ruling—from the imam, or check what a renowned mufti has said on a subject. The basic question *why* is not permitted in Islam, nor are critiques of the Prophet. As one writer put it, Islam demands "the assassination of the human mind." In Islam the goal is to submit to the guidance of the Prophet—not understand more of his love.

In contrast, the Christians I was getting to know weren't worried about getting everything right. They were pursuing a relationship with a Person, and that Person loved them dearly enough to give up his life for them. I began to wonder, *How much of what I have learned about both Islam and Christianity is wrong?* This was very difficult for me. It brought about an identity crisis. Could everything my family and society taught me about Islam and Christianity be untrue? My whole sense of reality and truth was collapsing right in front of my eyes. What would I do if my whole belief system were a lie?

The official penalty for apostasy from Islam is death. Most Westerners, and especially Muslims in the West, don't want to acknowledge this, but within the *hadiths* death is clearly prescribed as the punishment for a Muslim who apostatizes by becoming a Christian, Jew, or other religionist.[6] Granted, the death penalty is not always carried out for those who convert from Islam, but it is part of the sharia, and the more intensely Islamic the nation, the more likely that death will be meted out.[7] In Egypt, death was a real possibility if I were to convert. The death sentence might not be administered by the government but by the religious community. There have been cases where the secret police informed a radical Islamic group about converts in their midst so they could ferret them out and kill them.

I came to recognize that I would never become perfect by following all the rules of sharia. I could never be sure if my book of good deeds would be heavier than my book of evil deeds on Judgment Day, but I believed Christ could make me perfect. Since he was perfect, I could claim his perfection as my own if I accepted him. I was about to commit *shirk*, which is the unpardonable blasphemy of putting someone or something at the level of Allah, namely, Jesus Christ.[8] Would it be worth it? Should I risk death?

I didn't know what to pray or what to say, but I knew I had changed. The love of Christ had found me. One day I came across a copy of the *Four Spiritual Laws*, and in it I found the "Believer's Prayer." I prayed that prayer. I needed the love of Christ and his redemption, not merely warnings from the Prophet Muhammad. Jesus loved me; this I now knew.

I became a Christian, and on Christmas Day 1977 I was baptized into Christ. I chose the Christian name of Stephen, the first martyr, suspecting that my own martyrdom might not be far off.

CHAPTER FOUR

A
FRIGHTENED
NEW CHRISTIAN

I hid my new faith. When I went to church, I entered through the back door and left before the service was over. I told no one. In my third year of college, I had the opportunity to go to England for the summer, and took it. I worked in a Liverpool bakery, and sang along with a lot of Beatles music. While there I applied for religious asylum. But by the end of summer I hadn't received any news about my petition, and I decided to drop it.

So I went back to Egypt, where my family was starting to get suspicious. One obvious reason was my tongue. I had always had a sharp one and was quite an accomplished curser; I would curse your mother at the slightest provocation. My brother had often tried to cure me of my profanity by whacking his knuckles into my thighs when I cursed. Ouch! He never cured me, but after becoming a Christian I realized my tongue could not curse others at the same time that it praised God. My tongue was converted too.

I also started to get phone calls from my new Christian friends. In Egypt then—and to a lesser degree now—names themselves are enough to tell which religion a person professes. Christian boys were given names like Mark or Peter or Matthew. Muslim boys were named Mohammad or Ismail or Ali, and so on. So when I got calls from guys named Andrew and John, it aroused suspicion within my family. But they didn't really want to pursue it. As long as I didn't openly claim the Christian faith, I was still considered a Muslim. If you have a Muslim father, you are a Muslim, unless you openly convert. You need not profess your faith in Islam or be baptized or perform any other rite of initiation; you just follow the path of the Prophet (Sunna).

I joined a local Christian family for a Bible study in their home. A single Christian woman from my neighborhood attended as well. We got a ride back home from the father of the family, a local dentist. Since it would not be right for one woman to ride with two unrelated males, she asked one of her Muslim girlfriends to accompany her back home. Before departing, the dentist prayed to Christ for a safe journey, and along the way he talked about Christ with all of us, including the Muslim girl.

The latter was engaged to be married as soon as she finished college. Her fiancé's parents insisted that she finish college before they would provide her family with a dowry. She failed her final exams and had to spend another year in college. The likely cause of her failure was that she spent more time talking on the phone with her fiancé than she did studying. But somehow that wasn't what she told her parents. She told them that there were some Christians who had been harassing her, making it impossible for her to concentrate on her studies.

Her fiancé quickly found out and was furious that a Christian man was responsible for delaying their marriage plans for another year. He asked her who the infidel Christians were that had been proselytizing. She told him about her girlfriend who converted to Christianity and me. He knew exactly who I was since we grew up in the same town. He thought I was a Muslim and couldn't understand how I had been talking with her about Christ.

Now the trouble began. It all occurred in the month of Ramadan when Muslim feelings are heightened, as is their sensitivity about someone leaving Islam. The word began to spread that I had become a Christian. The fiancé came to talk with me and convince me of the error of my new way. But he didn't know much about either Islam or Christianity and was hardly persuasive. He brought along a cousin who was supposed to be well versed in the Qur'an to help unconvert me, but he wasn't much better.

Not long afterward, I was walking down a familiar street with a Coptic friend.[1] Some young men I knew accosted us in the street. "We're going to stone you, you infidel!" There were too many of them to run from or fight. I thought, *I'm dead*. I took off my glasses and said my final prayers. (I thought that the meaning of the name of Stephen would now become a reality.) One threw a stone at my feet, another at the dirt in front of his own feet.

"We're not finished with you yet!" they yelled. I was so scared that my heart was racing and my mind was imagining all kinds of scenarios for my death—hanging, having my throat slit, being stoned to death. But God protected us; no one even touched us. As Jesus said, "Even the hairs of your head are all numbered. So don't be afraid" (Matthew 10:30-31).

My Coptic friend was surprised, never having had such a scare. He had always been treated as a second-class citizen in Egypt, but since he had been raised Christian he had never been threatened with death. As an apostate from Islam, however, I was at far greater risk.

Unfortunately, the guys who threatened to stone me were true to their word. That night, in the midst of Ramadan, a dozen men came to our house. Among them were two of my dearest friends, who felt it their religious duty to participate. I was asleep, and my brother woke me up with the news that there were a lot people shouting downstairs wanting to kill me.

"Bring him out; we have to kill him!"

My brother Yasser went out on the porch to talk with them. He was by then well known in the neighborhood as a medical officer in the police hospital.

"You know what the law says, 'The apostate must be killed.'" My brother knew well enough what the law said. But given his stature in the neighborhood, he was able to disperse the crowd after a while.

"Leave him to me. I'm his older brother. I'll take care of this."

My brother came in and accosted me.

"Are you nuts? What do you think you are doing? You can't be serious!"

In stark contrast to my usual habit, I kept my mouth shut. The rest of the family, however, went wild.

"You are becoming a Christian! How could you put your family to such shame?"

"You claim that a man who drank and ate and slept like us was actually God?"

"You follow a religion that produces war criminals, from ancient times down to contemporary Ireland?"

"They can't even get the story of Jesus right; they need four tries with four Gospels."

"They can't add either. They think that one plus one plus one equals one in the Trinity. Are you crazy?"

"In fact, I think you are crazy. I'm taking you to a psychiatrist," said my brother.

I didn't know why at the time, but I objected. I later learned that some psychiatrists functioned as deprogrammers who would drug converts so they actually did become crazy.

My family told me they would not kill me, but they asked me to leave the house. So I packed my bag and was ready to go. But then they stopped me and said they would call the police instead. My brother called some acquaintances at the police station, and they soon came to pick me up. On the way I tossed a list of names and telephone numbers of fellow Christians into a canal. I didn't want them to end up in jail too.

Soon I found myself sitting in a stinking jail cell. There was no toilet; you had to take care of that in your own cell, as did the man next to you in his. They gave me the red-carpet treatment. That is, by the time they got done beating me the carpet was red with my blood.

As I sat, bleeding and bruised, in the dark and the stink, I asked myself, *What did I do wrong that I am being treated like a common criminal? Did I kill someone? Did I steal from someone? For what crime am I being punished?* If it were because of my belief I couldn't understand how my loving family could surrender me. In Arabic there are sayings about the closeness of family: "The blood never becomes water," for example, and "the fingernail will never leave the finger." But I felt that I had been abandoned and betrayed by those who were closest to me. Even so, the further away I felt from my family, the closer I felt to my Lord. After all, he said, "If they persecuted me, they will persecute you also" (John 15:20).

In the month of Ramadan you must fast every day. But every night you may eat, so most people eat a hearty meal before dawn, including the policemen in this station. So before they started fasting at dawn they began to interrogate me.

"Are you a Christian?"

"Do you really profess this silly business?"

"Are you a spy?"

They expected me to renounce the Christian faith and say that it was all a big mistake. They thought I was a good Egyptian kid who had been attracted to a Christian woman or perhaps offered money by Westerners to convert. Then they asked me the clinching question.

"Were you baptized?"

This was it. If you say you had merely been involved with some Christians, they might cut you some slack. But they recognized that baptism is crossing the line, the sign of full commitment to Christ.[2]

The words of Jesus in Matthew 10:32-33 kept ringing in my ears: "Whoever acknowledges me before others, I will also acknowledge before my Father in heaven. But whoever disowns me before others, I will disown before my Father in heaven."

"Yes, I have been baptized, and I am a Christian," I said.

They were quite surprised. They thought that, like most criminals, I would deny what I had done. According to sharia law I now had three days to repent and return to Islam. After that I would be declared an apostate, and anyone who killed me would be doing a favor to Islam. After three days I would be considered to be "behind the sun," the place of no return.[3]

They returned me to my brother and mother. My brother flat-out told me, "We won't harm you, but someone around here will. You have to get out of the house or you'll be killed."

I later learned that even the police who brought me home offered to have me killed. They couldn't do it openly since Egypt, like most other Muslim nations, affirms the United Nations Declaration on Human Rights, which includes religious freedom. So instead of killing me for my apostasy from Islam, they would see to it that I met with an unfortunate accident. The investigation of that accident would no doubt have yielded little evidence.

I was placed under house arrest. Every day someone would come to me to cure me of my craziness. First it was an imam, then a friend, then a Christian who had converted to Islam. They all said the same things, and they all failed to reconvert me. My brother's status in our neighborhood gave me a week rather than three days to disavow Christ.

My mother talked with me: "Son, I know what you must be going through. Why don't you just quietly keep what you have in your heart in your heart? But stay in our family. Go to the mosque and stay in Islam. Don't shame us."

She was right. I could have done that. Staying formally within Islam is not difficult. In fact, I suspect that many Muslims do just that. Follow the rules, recite the formal prayers, pay your tithe, and fast during Ramadan, and you appear to be a Muslim.

Instead, I refused to recant and was thrown out of the house. I had the clothes on my back and about five dollars in my pocket. I wandered around and made phone calls to my Christian friends. Finally I got ahold of a friend who picked me up and helped me find a place to stay. It took many hours since no one wanted to take me in. If they did, they would be, in effect, harboring a fugitive.

Finally, I found one Christian couple who was willing to help me. They got me out of Cairo and sent me to Alexandria—for my own safety. In Alexandria the Copts and other Christian groups have conferences on the Mediterranean for their own church members. I knew that if I went to these meetings, there would be no Muslim spies who might report me. I crashed conference after conference, ate their food, and stayed on their grounds. The Christians got to know me pretty well. I heard some excellent preaching and teaching, and made friends with many of them.

One Christian doctor from the Upper Nile (southern Egypt) invited me to move south and stay at a Christian facility there. But when we got there the director was not in, and I couldn't stay. So the doctor put me on a Christian speaking tour. As a new convert from Islam, I had a story that many wanted to hear, since most Christians in Egypt have been Copts for generations. When I spoke, other Muslims believed and came to Christ. I also earned a little income and was thrilled by the adulation of the Christian crowds. I was tempted to embellish my story to make a name and small fortune for myself, but did not. (Unfortunately, many converts get into this habit and never grow in Christ beyond this basic testimony.)

Finally I moved back to Cairo in order to finish my education. I could not live anywhere close to my old home, however, fearing for my life. I moved to a poor neighborhood on the other side of the city and roomed with another Christian, who was Roman Catholic. We both rented a room in an apartment from a third Christian, who was Pentecostal. At that time I didn't know that there were so many different groups within Christianity, so it was quite confusing. One night my Pentecostal landlord told me that I wasn't really a Christian because I had yet to be baptized in the Holy

Spirit and couldn't speak in tongues. I had no idea what he was talking about. I told him that I had taken classes in the "School of Tongues" (languages) in Cairo and could speak some English. I was confused, to say the least: if what he was telling me was true, I wasn't really a Christian. If that was the case, why was I enduring all this hardship for becoming a Christian? The Pentecostal man didn't stop with me. The next night he worked over the Roman Catholic man on the same issue.

Denominationalism has been a bane of the Christian mission among Muslims for many years. Islam, the Qur'an, and Allah are believed to be one solid whole, but Christianity looks like a jumble of competing, arguing sects. Muslims are attracted by the love of Christ, but then see animosity among different Christian denominations. Muslims do not convert to a denomination; they convert to Christ, but denominationalism often makes that difficult. Even today, when people ask me what denomination I belong to, I tell them that my former denomination was Islam but I am now a Christian. This response has left many speechless.

My dear mother never abandoned me. I got in touch with her, and told her where I was staying. She called me every week, and we would meet at my uncle's house. She cooked for me and delivered my favorite foods when we got together. A mother is always a mother; she always loves and cares, no matter what. I missed her, especially since we had become extremely close after my father's death. She would bring me blankets and other things I needed. Leaving my mother a couple of years later would be the hardest thing I ever did. She had raised me as a single parent for most of my life. She was a good, thoughtful, and devout person. But I could not ignore the words of Jesus when he said: "Anyone who loves their father or mother more than me is not worthy of me. . . .

Whoever does not take up their cross and follow me is not worthy of me. Whoever finds their life will lose it, and whoever loses their life for my sake will find it" (Matthew 10:37-39).

I was able to continue on in school since I was still in my third year of the business program, but I could no longer go to the university openly. So I got class notes from a couple of Christian women I had gotten to know, and studied the notes in our little apartment. Every other night I would trade sleeping spots with my fellow boarder; one night I got the bed and he the couch, the next we switched. I often got sick because I did not have the proper clothing or enough money for food. But on many occasions some of my Christian friends would come and give me money that they felt the Lord had called them to provide. My relationship with the Lord at that time was absolutely great. I felt as if he were so close I could touch him. There is nothing like persecution that will deepen a person's relationship with the Lord and demonstrate utter dependence on him. There really is no other option but to "trust and obey."

When it was time for my exams, I sat down at the desk with my number on it and took the tests. I talked with some other students afterward who had gotten the same balance on the accounting exam, and was confident that I had done well. But when the results were posted, I had failed. I would have to take the courses over again. How could that be? The reason they gave me was that I had been in the wrong examination room and wrong desk for my test. But that wasn't true. I had been very careful about getting to the right place at the right time, and I had heard my name called. A friend in the program later told me the real story. The dean told him, "That guy will not pass one class here while I'm the dean unless he returns to Islam." That dean later became the prime minister of

Egypt. He had earned his PhD from the University of Illinois, but had apparently not heard or accepted the gospel while he was there. What a shame!

I fell in love again. This woman was a fellow Christian convert and Egyptian I met in a Christian church. I wanted to get married, but an elder in the church told me he was not at peace about our marriage. For one thing, neither of us had jobs, and my outlook for getting one was nil. In fact, I not only had no job but no college degree either—and no money. I had disgraced my family and thus had no home, so I was hardly an ideal marriage prospect. With the church behind her, my new love rejected me.

Since I was still a third-year university student, I could apply again for a study abroad visa. The president of the Reformed Bible College in Grand Rapids, Michigan, had come to Cairo to do a series of lectures as a part of the Middle East Training Sessions, and I attended them. The RBC president, Dick Van Halsema, seemed to be impressed with me; I spoke quite a bit of English and had a good education. The pastor of my church recommended me for a scholarship to RBC. Dr. Van Halsema got back to us within a week. He made arrangements for me to get the scholarship to RBC, so I immediately applied for a US visa. That application, like most visa requests from single men in the Global South, was denied. Western nations are often suspicious of single young men who want an "education" in the West. They rightfully fear that a student visa is just an excuse to get into a Western country. So I was very grateful that a woman from our church who worked at the US Embassy in Cairo could pull some strings for me. I really did want to study and was accepted for a one-year student visa. Though this was not a long-term solution, it permitted me to escape my predicament in Cairo and continue my education.

Thanks to my church in Egypt, as well as other Christian friends, I could pay for the one-way ticket to the United States.

So I left my mother, my brothers, my sister, and my cousins without saying goodbye, lest anyone stop me from leaving. I left my neighborhood and schools. I left my friends. I left people who spoke Arabic. I left my country, my beloved Cairo, and my childhood faith. But I followed my Lord, Jesus Christ.

CHAPTER FIVE

In the
UNITED STATES

I am now a squat, often bearded, middle-aged Arab, and I have yet to be mistaken for Brad Pitt. After 9/11, when I have traveled in the United States, I am a suspect in most American airports. And when I come into the United States from trips abroad now, I am inevitably searched, questioned, and occasionally detained. The officer looks at my passport and sees an American name, Stephen; he looks at me and sees an Arab face. I am screened. More alarms go off than at a high school fire drill, since I've had knee surgery and now have titanium joints in my legs. I am questioned further. Calls are made. Welcome to the United States of America!

I had no such problems on my first trip. I was a young man of twenty-two, it was 1979, and no planes had crashed into the Twin Towers in New York. I landed in the United States on the Fourth of July, showed my student visa, breezed through customs, and saw fireworks going off.

"Was that for me?" I asked rhetorically. "Wow! What a great welcome!"

I couldn't get into the Reformed Bible College in Grand Rapids, Michigan, on that Fourth of July because no one was there to meet me, so I took a taxi to a hotel. The taxi driver pegged me as an innocent from abroad and took about an hour to drive six miles.

When school started, I found that my English wasn't nearly as good as it had seemed back home in Egypt. The vocabulary in psychology class was especially maddening; it didn't make sense to me even after I translated it. My education in Egypt had required rote learning, whereas my new school actually demanded that I think for myself. The professors were open to hearing from the students, whereas in Egypt the material was often presented in a very dry outline. The curriculum at RBC was what you would expect at a Bible college—lots of Bible with quite a few related subjects. I received a basic foundation in the Western liberal arts tradition. I learned the history, literature, and philosophy of the West. But it wasn't easy. There was no need for me to take the kind of business courses I had taken in Egypt and was most comfortable with.

My first year there I even had personal problems—such as gas. The processed and fatty foods in America simply did not compare to the fresh fruits and vegetables of Cairo. My innards rebelled. It got so bad that other students didn't even want to sit near me. I dearly missed my mother and my family. When in college in Egypt I had never lived in a dormitory; I had lived at home. So in a sense this was the first time I had lived away from home. Even though I was surrounded by other young Christians, I felt terribly lonely. Sometimes I just sat by a wall and cried.

Once I was safely established in Michigan, I sent my mother and siblings a letter explaining what had happened. They were shocked; yet, at the same time, they were relieved that I was okay.

They knew that every day I stayed in Cairo was a risk. My mother sent me money, fearing that I would starve if she didn't support me. She didn't know how little the Egyptian pound was worth in the United States, and I never told her. It was enough that she kept loving me, and her small donations reminded me of that love.

The first snowfall that winter in Michigan was a fantasy. To state the obvious—Cairo doesn't get much snow. I had heard of snow and had read about it in a few Bible passages, but the real stuff was amazing. Along with some other students, I joined in a snowball fight. I grabbed a white hunk and flung it at my roommate. Since I had had little practice at baseball, my aim was off. And since I had little experience with snow, I couldn't tell that I had grabbed a chunk of ice instead of snow. Replacing the dorm window I broke cost me ninety dollars. They took it from the small salary I earned working in the dining hall. It seemed like I was paying that bill off for months.

I often saw Dr. Van Halsema. Any time I needed to talk with someone I could drop in on him. The poor man heard all about my problems. He also hired me to do odd jobs around his house so I could have a little spending money. He even took me out to their family cottage on Lake Michigan.

I attended a local church in Grand Rapids. Every Sunday morning a family from the church, the Van Lopiks, picked me up from college and took me to church. I then stayed the afternoon with them. Since they were leaders of the young adults group at church, I went to those meetings on Sunday evenings. I became infatuated with the American women I met there and at school. Wow, they were wonderful, and they were Christian, so I could consider them as potential marriage partners. Following the Muslim courtship tradition that I had learned in Egypt, each time

I went out on a first date with a young woman, I explained my good intentions early on: that I was considering her as my future wife. Each time she promptly fled. Some friends, both male and female, tried to explain American dating protocol to me, but I never really got it. Finally, one wonderful young woman I met at the young adult ministry did not flee. That was Belinda, and I continued to court her even though her parents were suspicious of such a strange foreigner.

I also got to know Kent (not the coauthor of this book), a wonderful American pastor. That beautiful man wanted to do nothing but talk about Christ. He also happened to think that only the King James Version of the Bible provided the truth about Christ. When Kent's family learned of my situation as a foreigner on a student visa, they offered to adopt me, thinking that would enable me to live safely in the United States. They did so, which provided me with an American-sounding surname to go with my Christian name of Stephen.

The visa question soon came up, but the adoption didn't help. I had a one-year student visa that I couldn't get changed to permanent status, so I applied for religious asylum. When the State Department got the request, someone there must have looked at an official list of countries that practice religious persecution and found that it did not include Egypt. I knew all too well that the Islamic law of apostasy could cost me my life if I returned, but I couldn't find anyone to convince in the immigration court. I sat in front of the judge and pleaded. He had all the papers in front of him and was about to deport me. Finally, my adoptive father suggested that I demand the right to an attorney. I did, and my case started over. A generous church member hired a good attorney for me. That attorney got the case retried, and we won. So now I could legally stay in the United States as long as I wanted. The trial surprised me. In Egypt, the outcome of my case would likely have been arranged well in advance by friends or family connections, or by means of a healthy "gift." In the United States, however, an impartial judge actually looked at the case on its merits.

While this was going on, I continued my courtship with Belinda. I eventually proposed, and she accepted. She was also pregnant. When people learned that, they were doubly suspicious of my motives. They suspected that I had gotten her pregnant not only due to my lust but also so that I could get a visa. Nonetheless, we went forward with wedding plans. I borrowed some money for a ring, and still more money for a one-night honeymoon at a local hotel. We got married, and two men from RBC stood up as my groomsmen, one of whom was a fellow Egyptian. I lost track of him over time, but then met up with him years later when he was doing ministry in Jordan. Some months after our wedding, a beautiful healthy boy was born to Belinda and me in a Jewish hospital. We named him Nathaniel—gift of God.

I admit that my behavior with Belinda was not appropriate for a follower of Christ. In fact, before we married, we confessed our sin to the church. But after thirty-plus years of marriage, I think we have proved to the skeptics that I did not get her pregnant and marry her just to gain US citizenship.

After coming to RBC, I learned that none of my credits from the business school at the University of Cairo would transfer. But it was also becoming clear to me that I needed to dedicate my life to Christian ministry anyway, not business or diplomacy, as I had originally planned.

While at RBC, I was able to attend the Urbana 79 Student Missions Conference in Illinois. There I met young believers from all over the world. I still recall hearing John Stott give a series of daily devotionals from the book of Romans at that conference. Though his messages did not include a direct call to mission work, I knew the Spirit was leading me in that direction. The fact that there were thousands of other young people there who were eager to serve in missions no doubt confirmed this leading. I was now committed to working as a missionary among Muslims.

I had by now earned quite a number of credits at RBC, but I decided to transfer to the Cincinnati Bible College and Seminary, which accepted both my RBC credits and many of the credits I had earned at the University of Cairo. It took two more years to earn a master's degree in Middle Eastern history and archaeology there, and I relished studying a subject that was geographically and personally close to me.

Immediately after completing my MA, I wanted to get right into ministry among US Muslims. But I had a summer internship with a radio ministry based in Chicago called the Back to God Hour. There was a Lebanese preacher at that ministry named Bassam Madany, whose messages were broadcast throughout the Arab-speaking world. When listeners wrote to him for materials or advice, I and others would respond from the Chicago office. I got to know Dr. Madany quite well, and I respected his knowledge of both Christianity and the Arab world. When Dr. Madany learned that I wanted to go straight into ministry among Muslims, he took me aside and counseled me to go to seminary first. He appreciated my eagerness to get into ministry, but was sure that a good theological education would be better for me and my ministry in the long term. With a seminary education I would be well prepared for full-time ministry and would gain credibility in the North American church.

While we were in Chicago, my sister and her two children visited us. Since she worked for the United Nations, she had no trouble getting visas and was able to use her frequent-flyer miles to fly to the United States. While in my house, my sister had a little problem: she loves dogs, and we had one. However, the Prophet hates dogs—as do most Arabs. Muhammad even said that anyone who keeps a dog for purposes other than for protection or hunting would lose two points a day from his book of good deeds.[1] In Islam, dog saliva makes you impure and therefore incapable of attending prayers. If the dog licked my sister at any time during the day, she would become impure. What could she do? She called her imam back in Egypt and asked for a quick fatwa. The wise imam declared that she should keep one set of clothes for when she might be licked by my dog, after which she could wash, make a complete change of clothes, and be restored to ritual purity.

Twelve years after that visit, she admitted to me that while she was in our home in Chicago, she placed a spell on our house and hid an Islamic amulet in my closet. Upon her return to Egypt, she, my mother, my brothers, and an imam all sought my reconversion by means of that spell. After she confided this to me, I told her, "Jesus Christ protects his children from all these things." She admitted, "Yes, I guess so, you are still a Christian."

Before attending seminary I took another internship in Chicago through SCUPE (Seminary Consortium on Urban Pastoral Education). I worked in a community center in a pretty rough neighborhood. There were two leaders who had been missionaries to Muslims, Rev. Peter Ipema and Dr. Ray Tallman. Though I could not have known it at the time, those two men would be lifelong friends and mentors. This internship taught me about issues faced in urban ministries. Many of these issues had to do with money, insurance, and the health system. I learned about community banking, saw how social services worked, and gained a feel for what it was like to be a poor person in the rich United States.

I then went back to Michigan and attended Calvin Seminary, where I learned more about the Christian faith than I ever imagined possible. The studies were tough, but the biblical texts came alive for me. I understood much of the Old and New Testaments instinctively, since they were written from the perspective of a culture far closer to my own than that of my North American classmates. I read the Old Testament in Hebrew (which is very similar to Arabic) and the New Testament in Greek. I made friends with many of the students (one of whom is my collaborator on this memoir) and had some excellent professors. I remember having extensive conversations with a New Testament professor about the future role of Israel. I was pleasantly surprised to learn that a good scholar like him did not believe that the state of Israel would be the linchpin of God's plans for the church's future. I gained more knowledge about Christianity, which would later enable me to present Christianity to Muslims in a credible way.

Meanwhile, Belinda and I had another child, a girl. This one we also named after a Hebrew hero—Rebecca. The responsibility of another child, plus the strain of seminary studies, put some heavy pressure on our marriage. I was certainly not a typical American husband, and my wife was an adopted child who had gone through some identity struggles of her own. Her parents didn't think much of my indulgent Arab parenting style, and her mother had never really forgiven me for getting her pregnant. We were so poor that

Belinda's aunt gave us a quarter of a steer that was then butchered for us. We lived off of that meat for all our years in seminary. We were dependent on the charity of others and struggled emotionally, but with God's grace our family has stayed together.

CHAPTER SIX

MINISTRY
in the
UNITED STATES

In 1989 I was ordained as a minister and was sent to be a missionary among the Muslims in Dearborn, Michigan. The previous summer I had an internship in Ann Arbor, reaching out to the Arab students at the University of Michigan, so I knew that part of the state. Dearborn, just outside of Detroit, has the largest concentration of Arabs of any city in the United States, the vast majority of whom are Shia Muslims, or Shiites. Many had immigrated decades ago to work in the auto industry, and the Arab community has grown there ever since.

I began planting a church among the Lebanese Shiites, who were in the majority in our neighborhood. Having been raised as a Sunni Muslim, I even had a culture shock of my own when I got to know how dissimilar these strains of Islam were. The Shiites do not accept any of the hadiths (sayings) from Muhammad's followers or those of his wife, Aisha; they only accept those that were spoken by the prophet himself. The Shiites believe that Muhammad's cousin and son-in-law, Ali, should have been named his immediate successor. Ali did eventually become the fourth "rightly guided caliph" of Islam, but only after Abu Bakr, Omar, and Uthman preceded him. During the reigns of the first three caliphs, Aisha, Muhammad's youngest wife, opposed Ali. He did eventually rule, but Hussein, who was the son of Ali and Muhammad's daughter, Fatimah, was killed by a successor of Omar in the battle of Karbala (Iraq).[1] This direct physical line of Muhammad later died out, but many Shiites believe that a twelfth-generation descendant of Ali, the *Mahdi* (or hidden imam) will return at the end of time.

One night I had a discussion with some Shiite friends about the differences among Sunnis, Shiites, and Christians. We argued and argued over a point in a hadith. Finally, at 2 a.m. they called their imam for a ruling on the question we were debating. He grumpily got out of bed, heard their question, and then said that my position was correct. I gained a bit of credibility that night.

Most Shiites are from Iran and Iraq.[2] As a rule, they are better educated than the Sunnis, so it was pleasant to converse with them about all things religious. They also believe that it is possible to have contemporary interpretations of the Qur'an, and are thus a bit more open to discussions about new things in religion than are most Sunnis.[3] Nonetheless, I knew that I could not speak with them directly about Christ until I earned the right to be a part of their lives. So I got to know them socially and became involved in their families. In order to help them adapt to life in the United States, I often served as their translator. When they got documents in English that they didn't understand, they would bring them to me. When they needed to go to court for something, I came along as their interpreter. One or two judges came to recognize me as the local Arabic translator. Of course, picking an Egyptian with a clerical collar out of the crowd was hardly a feat of great perception.

Our family and a few Christian friends tried to get to know as many of the Arabs in Dearborn as possible. There were Yemenis, Lebanese Shiites, Iraqi Sunnis, Chaldeans, and Palestinians from Ramallah. In fact, there are more Palestinians from the hot spot of Ramallah in Dearborn today than there are in Ramallah itself.

To reach these Arabs, we would sometimes show the *Jesus* film or other Christian movies in the park at night. To do so, we had to get a permit, ask the guard to open and close the gate for us, set up equipment, and so on. As it turned out, the park guard saw our movies more than anyone else. He also saw that we were Christians from various ethnic groups who treated one another respectfully. He was a Lebanese man who knew what Muslims were doing to one another in the civil war in Lebanon at the time. So when he saw a movie that told of God's love for all and saw it practiced among us, he cried—and he accepted Christ.

We didn't build an edifice since I knew that a church building would scare off most Muslims. Instead, we developed an Arab Community Center modeled on the community center where I had interned in Chicago. In addition to doing translations, we taught English, helped people with bills and immigration papers, and sponsored a number of social gatherings. I wanted to do holistic ministry. I knew that merely preaching at them would remind them of all the bad things they had heard about Christians.

I was once asked to go to a social services office as a translator for some Arabs. A woman who had lost her job, along with her elderly mother, went to claim welfare services. I knew them both fairly well. They owned a house in which they lived on the lower floor, and they collected rent from a family who lived on the upper floor. So the welfare agent asked all the usual questions—name, addresses, number of family members, and so forth. Then he asked, "Any income other than that of your job?" The woman said, "Why no, you can ask Stephen." As a good Arab friend, I should have said, "No, there is no other income." One Arab can't make another look like a liar or a cheat. But as an American who was trusted by this government agency in Dearborn, I knew I should report the cash they got paid for the rent. I was stuck. I finally managed a wry smile and directed it at the agent. He understood. When we left the office I told the women I would never again translate for them, and if they tried any similar shenanigans, I would report them.

We provided social services for both Christians and Muslims. In Islam, you are required to take care of poor Muslims via the almsgiving (*zakat*), but you do not have responsibility for believers from other faiths. And even the zakat doesn't provide much care for many Muslims. Muslim nations are among the poorest in the world, to which the massive slums of Cairo are a depressing testament. Wealthy Arabs or Arab nations often do very little for the poor though they are all part of the one great House of Islam (Dar al-Salam). So when Christians care for the Muslim poor, we show them love that they often don't receive from their own people. It is often startling to them that someone who does not share their faith is concerned about them and helps them.

We invited many Arab friends into our home. When we did, Belinda would prepare *halal* (Islamically acceptable) Muslim foods and drinks for them. We would sometimes throw birthday parties for our kids and theirs, with clowns, games, and popcorn. We wanted to show them that they could indeed be Arab, Christian, and American.

I would meet many Arab men while they were at work. Most gas stations in Dearborn seem to be owned by Arabs, so every time I filled up I would make a point of talking to the man who managed the station. Plenty of good restaurants are run by Arabs as well, so I gained some girth as I evangelized.

Detroit and Dearborn were very racially polarized cities at that time. The racial divisions were especially sharp between blacks and Arabs. Most Arabs see the blacks as inferior, call them *a'bede* (slaves), and are surprised that they must live alongside them as equals in the United States. Many blacks see the Arabs as greedy leeches that suck up the business opportunities in their neighborhoods and then overcharge for their services. I tried to explain to the Arab shopkeepers I came in contact with that the racism they had been raised with in the Middle East was not correct. All are children of God, regardless of racial origin. But old habits die hard, and prejudices remain. Like many ethnic groups, Arabs typically establish enclaves in which only their own are welcome.

Having come from the Middle East, I assumed that soccer would be the game of preference among teenagers. I soon found out that the Arab kids in Dearborn wanted to play basketball instead. So we started a basketball team among local Arab teens, and played in a Catholic school gymnasium. We started with about four kids, but then grew to about sixteen. After the games we would go to Burger King for some non-halal food. These kids wanted to be American. They changed their names from Ibrahim to Abe, from Muhammad to Mike, and Mahmoud to Moe. We talked about life in the United States and about the Christian faith. A number of these young men accepted Christ.

While in Dearborn I trained some Americans who were going to serve as missionaries in Islamic lands. I thought that Americans wouldn't know anything about missions to Muslims, but they had incredible success. Each summer some of them came to work with us. These American missionaries started to play baseball with the Arab kids. This became so popular that the kids would wait in line at the ballpark for a chance to play baseball. This gave me an opportunity to sit with the parents in the stands and talk with and minister to them.

In 1989, while we were living in Dearborn, my dear mother came to visit us. My sister had made the flight arrangements for her, typed them up, laminated them, and hung them as a pendant on her necklace. She went from Cairo to London to New York to Detroit to see her youngest and apostate son. I'm told that in New York she made a real nuisance of herself by shouting, "Detroit, Detroit!" at the desk attendant, since she was so scared she might miss that last flight. As an Arab woman, she was also mad that she had to ride in a cart driven by an African American man at the airport.

When she arrived in Detroit, I met her at the airport and cried. She was a wonderful mother, and I hadn't seen her in twelve years. I was now married, had two children, and two academic degrees. We talked incessantly for two weeks straight. She caught me up on all the events in the family that we really couldn't do via the mail. For many years she had harbored the hope that I might return to her faith and her home. But after all this time she had come to realize that my conversion to Christianity was no passing fad. I talked with her about my Christian faith, and she was largely receptive to it. I made a few comments about some problems in Islam, and she agreed. But when it came to accepting Christ as part of the Trinity, her Muslim foundations could not be shaken. No, no man can really be God.

As hard as it had been for her to accept my new faith, it was probably harder for her to accept my new name. How could I deny who I really was? Was I ashamed of her and family? I explained as gently as possible that the change to an American name was a legal necessity due to my adoption. I assured her that I was proud as could be about my family, and that I would remain part of it till the day I died.

It didn't occur to me at the time that talking to my mother in Arabic all day wouldn't be the best thing for our marriage. I soon learned, however, that ignoring my wife while talking to my mother in Arabic was not what a marriage counselor might recommend. As I left each day to work in the church, my mother would stay home with Belinda and the children. My mother knew no English and my wife knew no Arabic. The only sounds my wife understood were mother's "tsk, tsk, tsk" that she spoke while scolding the children for their little mistakes. I eventually realized my own mistake, and I stopped leaving them alone together with no means to communicate. Though for fun, I will still sometimes wag my finger and say, "tsk, tsk, tsk," in imitation of my mother when I want to tease my wife.

As a male, I could not communicate openly with the Arab women in Dearborn, so I was glad when a Lebanese Christian woman joined me in ministry. She was an evangelistic superstar. She worked with the local women and brought many to Christ. As a woman, she could meet with them in their homes without anyone else around, and she was fearless about proclaiming the faith. I have found that women are often stronger believers than men. Since then she has started centers modeled on our own in four other US cities.

While in Dearborn I pulled off a coup of Protestant ecumenism. I got the Baptist, Presbyterian, Christian Reformed, and Missionary Alliance churches to work together. They all were supportive of our ministry to Muslims. I hoped that the Dearborn Muslims would not be as confused about Christian denominations as I had been. I also became part of the Detroit Leadership Network, an ecumenical prayer group that included Detroit area politicians, and business and religious leaders. The mayor of Dearborn at that time was Michael Guido, a devout Catholic. Instead of calling his office with complaints and problems, which is what he heard most, I called asking how I could best pray for him and his work.

During the first Gulf War, the Arab community was deeply divided. Jews from the local synagogues had placed a well-reasoned position statement in the Dearborn and Detroit newspapers explaining the Israeli position on the war, and I thought the Arab community should do the same. No such luck. Many of us wanted to condemn Saddam Hussein for his unprovoked attack on the Kuwaitis. But the Yemenis hated the Kuwaitis, and were glad to see Hussein go after them. The Palestinians also liked Saddam since he had given them money to support their cause of statehood. The Iraqis who had fled to the United States hated Saddam, but they didn't want to see Iraq attacked. One unfortunate Iraqi mother even had one son in the US army and another in the Iraqi army. It was a lesson to Americans—and to me—that Arabs are not all alike in their politics.

Hussein is a very common name among Arabs, especially among the Shiites, since Hussein was the name of Muhammad's grandson from the line of Ali. During the Gulf War some Americans would flip through the Dearborn phonebook and call up anyone named

Hussein. They would harass that person and ask if he was related to the madman from Iraq. Or they would tell him to get out of the United States or else they would attack him. Some citizens of Dearborn even suspected that the Arabs might poison the drinking water. The FBI once visited me during this time, asking whether I knew of any conspiracies. I did not.

While we lived in Dearborn, a Muslim friend of mine, Muhammad, came to me and asked me to help one of his relatives. One of his cousins was going through a divorce, and she feared losing both her home and her children. Her husband, a lower-level imam at the local mosque, was trying to take the house away from her. He thought that if he could show she had no income, he could prove that he ought to get the house and the kids. After meeting with her, we learned that she had enough money for one more month's mortgage payment. Since she could ante up the first month's payment, social services in Dearborn would provide the second. We got her on her feet financially, and she was able to keep the house and kids. This did not please her husband. He knew I was involved and soon started rumors about his ex-wife and me— which were totally untrue. Knowing how easily such sparks could roar into a blaze, I made sure I was never once left alone with her, or, for that matter, with any other woman. In fact, she was often together with my wife and family, and saw how we got along as a couple.

Nevertheless, the sparks of the rumors kindled into a blaze. I had to do something or my reputation would be ruined, as well as any hope for a church. I went to the senior imam at the mosque and said to him: "Look, let's set aside questions of religion: I know you are an imam, and you know I am a Christian pastor. But among us Arab men, is there anything more important than maintaining the honor of your good name?"

He agreed, as I knew he would. Our Arab culture sees dishonor as the worst of conditions.

"Your junior imam has gone around lying about me," I said, "making my name stink throughout the whole Arab community. You know what he has done against his wife, and you know what he is trying to do with their house and kids. Please make him stop before the shame touches us all."

I don't know exactly what he did to or told the junior imam, but the rumors abruptly stopped. Not only did the negative stories cease, but positive comments began circulating about the crazy Egyptian pastor who cared more about the imam's family than the imam did. I felt as Joseph did with his brothers: "You intended to harm me, but God intended it for good" (Genesis 50:20). Instead of seeing my name shamed throughout the community, my name—and more importantly, Christ's name—was honored.

During the celebration of *Eid* that year, that senior imam gave me a beautiful Arabic-English Qur'an. At Thanksgiving the following year, I reciprocated with a halal turkey plus an Arabic-English Bible. I wrote a few verses on a card about why Thanksgiving is celebrated in the United States. Since he had given me a beautiful gift earlier, he accepted mine with gratitude. He did not turn to Christ, but he is an example of how Muslims can relate comfortably to Christians in the West.

My brother Yasser also visited us while we lived in Dearborn. He was quite successful in his medical career, and money was certainly not an issue for him. Since he is my oldest brother, he felt responsible for the fact that I converted to Christianity on his watch. So he came to Dearborn on a mission: he wanted to bring me back home and back to Islam. He had selected four books to take with him to my home; they were all Muslim attacks on Christianity. But before he had a chance to sway me, he had a heart attack in our home. We raced him to the emergency room at a local hospital. I stayed with him overnight, and it was an honor to care for my elder brother in that hospital room. Belinda also stayed with him, bathing and caring for him. He was moved by this, but not to the point of accepting Christ.

When he returned to Egypt, he continued to seek medical treatment for his heart. Since he was the chief medical officer in a Cairo hospital, he knew some of the world's leading specialists. At that time the world's leading heart specialist was Magdi Yacoub, who was an Egyptian and a Coptic Christian. As a Christian he could not get ahead in Egypt, so he immigrated to England. He became so well recognized there that he was knighted by the queen. My brother had previously invited Magdi to Egypt for seminars and conferences. So when he needed triple bypass surgery, he traveled to England and had his friend Magdi perform it there.

Today, as seen in my own family, there is a far greater amount of transit between Muslims and Christians than there has been for centuries. Many Arabs and Westerners can travel freely into each others' countries. The increase in contact between Western Christians and Arab Muslims will continue and grow. There are some places in the United States where Muslims are scarce, but perhaps not as many as you might think. Major universities and international businesses usually include Muslims, and there are areas in the United States, such as Dearborn, where they are in the majority. I hope that Americans will not be afraid of Muslims, suspecting them of being terrorists. Rather, my prayer is that Muslims find open hearts and homes among the Christians here.

CHAPTER SEVEN

ARABS
and the
WEST

Once, when I returned to Dearborn from England after the 9/11 attacks, I was driving a borrowed car that someone from a neighboring church had lent me and noticed a police officer behind me. I started sweating.

He flashed his lights, so I pulled over. He told me that the license plate had passed its renewal date. He asked me for my driver's license. When I showed it to him, he looked at it for a long time. I sweated profusely. He asked me for the insurance and registration cards. I couldn't find either one. I was now dripping with sweat. I was an Arab; I was in someone else's car, with an American name on the driver's license and no insurance and registration shortly after 9/11. Was I facing deportation, jail, or perhaps interrogation by the CIA?

Miraculously, the cop believed at least some of what I told him and let me off with a ticket for driving with an expired tag on the license plate. When I returned the car to my friend, he apologized for failing to put the insurance and registration forms in the glove compartment—but then enjoyed a long, hearty laugh at my expense.

I saw the 9/11 attacks as being ideologically driven. Look at the buildings the bombers destroyed. The Twin Towers were citadels of capitalism and included many powerful financial institutions. The other building hit was the Pentagon, the headquarters of the American military. The plane that was brought down in Pennsylvania was headed toward the White House, the summit of American political power. Al Qaeda wanted to make a point that many Arabs empathize with: "We hate the fact that you have power over us."

The West, and especially the United States, holds military, political, media, technological, and economic power over most of the world. For Arabs raised on stories of the Golden Age of Islam, the fact that they now live in third-class conditions in the world's poorest nations is shameful. They hear the call to prayer five times a day saying, "Hasten to prayer, hasten to prosperity," and wonder what went wrong. They believe that Allah is the one true God, and that his people should thus be the most prosperous. But the Western "Christian" nations are clearly more successful than Islamic lands. As a result of this constant sense of humiliation, many Arabs cheered Al Qaeda on 9/11, feeling that the arrogance and power of the West had finally been challenged.

Some years after 9/11, one American Christian woman asked me, "Why should we help the Arabs when they want to kill us?" I was torn. As an Arab, I felt bad that my fellow Arabs had indeed killed innocent Americans. I also felt bad that Americans would look at me as a likely terrorist simply because I am an Arab. When I first saw the television pictures of the planes hitting the Twin Towers, my immediate thought was, "I hope it's not an Arab who did this." But it was, and the history of the West and the Middle East is irreversibly changed.

I also hope Americans recognize that not all of "them" (Arabs) are of one mind. Not all Arabs supported the attacks, and most are far more envious of the West than hostile to it. Arabs do not have any more of a genetic tendency toward violence than do Norwegians, Americans, or Spaniards. I grant that *jihad* has long been part of Islamic tradition since its beginning. But jihad is not seen as necessary by most Muslims in most cases, and it can also be interpreted as the inner struggle that every believer faces. The radicals who called on young Arab men to become suicide bombers are abusing the tradition of jihad.

On the religious side of this issue, I responded to the questioning woman this way: Christ simply demands that we "love our enemies." Even if someone persecutes you, Christ demands that we respond with his love for that person. The gospel has rarely gone out to friends of Christ; far more often it has been presented to his enemies. Many missionaries have suffered, and some have been martyrs. Most North Americans, however, don't want to remember that persecution has long been common among those who go forth as Christian missionaries.

The church in the West seems to have lost its willingness to suffer for the sake of Christ, not recognizing that persecution is a natural event for Christians. Jesus himself talked about persecution as a normal consequence for those who leave their families and homes for the sake of the gospel (Mark 10:29-31). St. Paul also wrote, "We are God's children. Now if we are children, then we are heirs—heirs of God and co-heirs with Christ, if indeed we share

in his sufferings in order that we may also share in his glory"
(Romans 8:16-17). Yet many Americans seem to think that if
someone is suffering for the cause of Christ, it is an abnormality
and must be stopped. It is not. Suffering is a part of the normal
Christian life in much of the world. American Christians could
learn a great deal about the cost of following Christ from their
Arab brothers and sisters.

Arabs in the United States often have family in their home
countries and keep in close contact, so things that happen in the
Middle East have tremendous effect on them. Many Muslims are
deeply ashamed of the violence of their fellow Muslims toward
Westerners and to one another. They see that Al Qaeda kills fellow
Muslims as well as Westerners. They saw Sunni and Shiite Muslims
kill one another with poison gas in the Iraq-Iran War, and later
engaged in civil war in post-Saddam Iraq. They hear of Sunni
versus Shiite warfare in Syria and know that Muslims have long
warred among themselves and hated one another. After the Arab
Spring they not only suspected but learned for a fact that their
leaders were corrupt, and they know that many Muslims have experienced oppression at the hands of their own governments. By
comparison, Arabs in the United States can't help but notice that
the United States does not make war on its own people and generally tries to take care of its poor. They see that things really work
in the United States: roads are repaired, purchases are made without
bribes, and families live together in peace. Most Arabs in America
are relieved to be here.

Nonetheless, Muslims in the West are often stuck between two
worlds. They do not fit well in Western culture, and often do not
want to. They want to keep their Arab and Muslim identity, and
maintain their distinctive minority status. As a result they are often

even more conservative than their brothers and sisters who still live in the Middle East.

I was once in the home of an American Muslim who had seen our video titled *God's Love*. He appreciated it and wanted to know more about Christianity. While we were together, his cousin from the Middle East came to visit. When the cousin heard what we were talking about, he started to shout verses from the Qur'an that contradicted Christianity. Though my friend was not then a Christian, he stood up to his cousin and talked to him about the things he had learned from the movie. He was a very conservative Muslim but would not let me, his friend, be insulted in his home.

In general, the United States and the European nations are afraid to confront Islam. The politically correct demand for tolerance silences most real dialogue and critique. The writings of some Arab scholars, such as Edward Said (d. 2004), have characterized legitimate historical and literary critiques of Islam as though they were racist attacks. Some have labeled anyone who questions or critiques Islam—even an Arab Muslim convert like myself—as "Islamophobic." The history of Islam is being rewritten in a way that avoids its bloody and unjust aspects, including its widespread denigration of women. Recent translations of the Qur'an, for example, often soften its violent and sexist passages. Prestigious universities in the United States and Europe endow Islamic chairs, often financed by wealthy Muslims. The scholars sitting in these academic chairs present an air-brushed view of Islam to the West. It is a sad irony that though cultures in the West have waged war and fought enormous legal battles to gain freedoms of speech, conscience, and religion, they do not use those freedoms to address Islam critically and openly.

One small example of how freedoms go in only one direction is Fordson High School in Dearborn. During the time we lived there, the school went from being majority Anglo to majority Muslim. When the Muslims were a minority, the cafeteria would make halal food for them. When the majority became Muslim, they demanded that the cafeteria serve only halal food, and they forbade students from playing any sports on Fridays. The then-minority Anglos had to eat the Muslims' food and conform to their wishes about the Muslim sabbath.

The US media are of little help. They typically depict Muslims and Arabs as either terrorists or wealthy sheiks with harems. Seeing this, North Americans who watch or listen to the media often come away with a skewed view of what Islam is. To my surprise, I learned that few Americans can spell Qur'an, mention the five pillars of Islam, or name the century in which the Prophet lived. I don't know who said it, but the aphorism "If you think education is expensive, just try ignorance" is certainly true of America's ignorance about Islam.

This is despite the fact that radical Islam has challenged the United States and will continue to do so. Radical Islam seeks to get back to its Golden Age. It sees secularization and Christianization as equally horrible and heretical options. In this sense, radical Islam is more consistent with the Qur'an and the hadiths than is modernized Islam. The radicals want everything to be Islamic, just as it was in its Golden Age. At that time sharia law was the law of the land, the rulers were Muslim caliphs, and the imams rendered legal judgments for the whole people (umma). There was but one God and one rule in the land. Jihadists today are willing to die in order to bring back those good old days. In fact that is often their cry: "Come back to the true faith!"

During the recent Arab Spring, Egyptians were disappointed that it took so long for the United States to come to their aid. President Obama continued to support President Mubarak long after Egyptians demanded his ouster. My brother Muhammad was among the protestors in Tahrir Square, and felt the antipathy expressed toward the United States. The lack of support from the West confirmed our suspicion that the United States is really more concerned with its own wealth and oil supplies than it is in justice and democracy for all.

US politicians and even presidents are often uninformed about Islam. For example, on September 17, 2001, when the smoke was still rising from the rubble in New York and Washington, DC, President George W. Bush made the incredible statement that "Islam is peace." This is not true. *Islam* means "submission," and often submission of the boot-on-your-throat variety.[1] How could the president say this one week after watching the Twin Towers burn? Had he ever read more than a page of the history of Islam? Military jihad has been a part of Islam since Muhammad moved from Mecca to Medina and began fighting the neighboring Arabs, Jews, and Christians who would not accept his political-religious authority.

While the United States was saying that Islam is peace, it was at the same time sending Muslim prisoners of war to Islamic states that practice torture. The Egyptian secret police and other similar groups have few qualms about torturing their enemies. So prisoners from Iraq and Afghanistan were apparently outsourced to these nations, where the dirty work was done. This too affects how Muslims view the West and its religion. To Muslims the West is the Christian West: it is decadent, arrogant, and violent. In contrast,

Muslims see themselves as the pious ones who humbly pursue the will of God.

As a result of all the cultural and political issues between Middle Eastern Muslims and Western Christians, mission work is often very slow, as it was for us. I realized that I needed to build relationships before I could do any evangelism, and that took time. Unfortunately, the mission agency I worked with then firmly believed in the "three selves" of church development: they believed that a mission church should be self-sustaining, self-governing, and self-propagating within five years. After five years the work I had begun in Dearborn was not able to support itself in these ways, so the agency pulled the plug on our ministry.[2]

At just that time, the international director of Arab World Ministries, Dr. Ray Tallman, who I knew from Chicago, was hoping to find someone with expertise in the Arab world to serve as a trainer for missionaries. This person would need to have theological training in Christianity as well as an understanding of Islam and the Arab culture. Most of his team thought that no such person could be found. But Dr. Tallman knew me well, since I had worked under him years earlier in Chicago. He also knew that my English had developed to near fluency, and that I had a good rapport within my American church. He had kept track of me and came to Dearborn to visit. We were later interviewed by six members of AWM, and unanimously approved for the position. I was to be their "Islamist at large." My role would be to help the Western missionaries understand Islam and the Arab world.

Belinda and I prayed and asked the Lord's guidance. I was afraid we would not be able to raise enough support to make the move. So in order to make a little extra money, I cleaned offices and bathrooms in Detroit. We put our house up for sale in Dearborn, and within five days we had five offers. We needed a place to stay for two more months, so we rented our own home from the new owners. Since we got a high offer so quickly, we saw it as a green light from the Lord: Go to London.[3]

Thankfully, the church in Dearborn that supported us provided us with a severance package that kept our family afloat financially. We had peace about the decision to move, and are still supported by that wonderful church.

CHAPTER EIGHT

In
EUROPE

O ur family moved to England in 1996. Nathaniel was fourteen and Rebecca was twelve. For a time, we lived two hours south of London in an apartment, but then moved to our own house in Worthing. One single ministry supporter in England gave us enough money to make the down payment on our house. She was the same woman who first welcomed us when we interviewed for the position. Her husband was a banker in London and Hong Kong, and they had no children.

Rebecca resisted the move initially, but she adjusted to it quite quickly. We promised that we would get her a dog once we got to England, which we did. Nathan and Becky both went to Church of England schools, Nathan in an all-boys school, and Becky in an all-girls school. They each had to wear their school's special uniforms.

We visited various churches in the area, but we didn't want to be recognized as yet another American couple working for Arab World Ministries. We finally settled in a Church of England congregation a short distance away, where many of our children's classmates were members. We stayed in that good church for fourteen years. I eventually became part of the leadership team, and preached there three or four times a year. Given the emphasis on sacramental theology in the Anglican Church, I was not permitted to administer the Eucharist, but we made many friends there and grew our family in that church. We also raised the level of interest in ministry among Muslims there and in other churches. This interest, however, was not shared by the British government. In their eyes, our evangelistic efforts among Muslims broke the code of religious tolerance that most of the English had grown up with.

I led conferences and evangelistic meetings in Holland, Germany, Sweden, and elsewhere among Arab immigrants. I sometimes spoke with these European Muslims for hours and even days on end. Some of the Muslim conferees got angry with me for challenging Islam, but others were quite interested in what I had to say. My policy was to be ready for any and all questions, and to consider all of them legitimate. I would respond to their questions about Islam and Christianity from only the most respected sources for each. For example, since some hadiths have less respect than others, I would use only those that were acknowledged by the highest authorities in Islam. After a typical five-day conference, it was not unusual for 150 of the 250 conferees to accept Christ!

This was tremendous. It was and is the highlight of my life. God has given me the opportunity to help lead hundreds of Muslims to faith in Christ. I know that many missionaries have worked among Muslims for decades without seeing any fruit of their labor. The success I have experienced shows that many Muslims are hungry to hear about Christ, though most won't admit it. Since they are away from the Middle East, they can openly seek out Christians or raise questions about Islam that they would not dare to in their countries of origin.

My job with Arab World Ministries not only allowed me to travel throughout the Middle East, but demanded that I do so. I was tasked with supporting all the missionaries sent by Arab World Ministries. I met some of them in London when they were home on furlough, and I met others at seminars throughout the Middle East and North Africa. Most of them worked with established churches in the region. By teaching them about Islam and Arab culture, I showed them how to relate to Muslims and Arabs.

For me this was a great opportunity to learn as well. When I was in Dearborn, I learned a great deal about the Shiites, both through personal experience and study. When traveling from London to various locations in the Middle East, I learned how big and diverse the world of Islam is. For example, in the North African nation of Mauritania, the people are divided about equally between blacks and Arabs. All are Muslims. Yet the two racial groups don't intermarry, don't attend the same mosques, and don't have much to do with each other in general. Though they are united by both religion and nationality, they are divided by race. Many Arab countries are like this: ethnic differences trump religious unity. I realize that the West is hardly free of racism, but Christianity can be. In Christianity there is "no Greek or Jew, slave or free, male or female," but all are one in Christ. Even the detractors of Christianity realize that it has spread throughout the globe to the point that it now includes people of virtually all races, tongues, and cultures.

When training missionaries, I tried to help them understand what to do and what not to do in their Muslim contexts. In general, I urged the missionaries to respect Islam and the Muslims, without challenging their faith directly. Rather, I encouraged them to show

Christ's love to them in many different ways. This runs counter to the Western tendency to win arguments or to point out the flaws in the other person's viewpoint. But that approach is often seen as an insult by most Muslims, and it almost never leads them to Christ. Muslims see the West as anti-Muslim, and they are extremely sensitive if they perceive they are being belittled or insulted. Showing them the love of Christ in concrete ways, by inviting them to meals or showing care for them and their families, is a far more fruitful strategy.

While we were in England in June 2007, Salman Rushdie was knighted by Queen Elizabeth. Rushdie is a renowned literary figure, and as an Indian was a member of the British Empire. He had written many books and won many literary awards, including the Booker Prize. He was raised as a Muslim but became quite secular in his adulthood. The book that made him infamous among Muslims is *The Satanic Verses*, published in 1988. Rushdie did not draw his book's title out of thin air. The verses do not now occur in the Qur'an but were referred to in sura 53 and are acknowledged by leading Islamic scholars.[1] They report a time when Muhammad was tempted to worship the gods of his old polytheistic Arab tribe, the Quraysh. The Quraysh wanted Muhammad to worship their three Arabian goddesses, Al-Lat (the female parallel to Allah), Al-Uzza, and Manat, in return for their own worship of Allah. Muhammad agreed. This delighted the Quraysh and made it appear that reconciliation was possible between Muhammad and his estranged tribe. But in a later vision the angel Jibril (Gabriel) rebuked Muhammad for his fall from pure monotheism and insisted that he never again recognize any God but Allah. Muhammad then withdrew the verses from the Qur'an. A later Qur'anic vision explains what had happened when he received the tempting satanic verses: "We sent not ever any Messenger of Prophet before thee, but that Satan cast into his fancy, when he was fancying; but Allah annuls what Satan casts, then Allah confirms His signs—surely Allah is all-knowing, All-wise" (sura 22:52).

This explanation says that earlier prophets too had been misled by Satan. In fact, it seems to suggest that this satanic temptation actually authenticates Muhammad's status as a true prophet, making him even more reputable. It also serves as an example of the process of abrogation, in which a later verse from the Qur'an abrogates an earlier one. This text has long been problematic for Islamic scholars since it raises questions about the authenticity of Muhammad's monotheism, the nature of revelation in the Qur'an, and the Prophet's ability to distinguish between true and false revelation.

Rushdie took this highly problematic passage from Islamic history as the centerpiece of his narrative. In *The Satanic Verses*, the lead character has a series of visions much as Muhammad did. One vision includes a heathen princess, a radical skeptic, and a satirical poet; these serve as parallels to the three goddesses of the Quraysh. In that same vision, the satirical poet moves to a house of prostitution where the prostitutes have the names of the prophet's wives, a clear sacrilege. In another dream, a young peasant girl receives visions and is told to cross the Arabian Sea and make a pilgrimage to Mecca with her people. The people disappear as they attempt to cross the sea, but it is unclear whether they drowned or were miraculously transported to Mecca, perhaps mimicking Muhammad's mysterious Night Journey to Jerusalem. Still another dream presents a crusty imam who bears an uncanny resemblance to the Ayatollah Khomeini himself.

Tampering with the Qur'an is not appreciated in Islam, to put it mildly,[2] and blasphemy is a capital offense. Saying anything negative about the Prophet is forbidden, especially by non-Muslim speakers. So Rushdie had done the unspeakable. In 1989 the Ayatollah Khomeini of Iran issued a death sentence on Rushdie, and that sentence has been renewed by his successors. Rushdie has survived in hiding in England and later in the United States, but others, including one of his translators, were killed. Here is the report of the deaths that resulted from the publication of *The Satanic Verses*.

With police protection, Rushdie escaped direct physical harm, but others associated with his book have suffered violent attacks. Hitoshi Igarashi, his Japanese translator, was stabbed to death on 11 July 1991. Ettore Capriolo, the Italian translator, was seriously injured in a stabbing in Milan on 3 July 1991. William Nygaard, the publisher in Norway, was shot three times in an attempted assassination in Oslo in October 1993, but survived. Aziz Nesin, the Turkish translator, was possibly the intended target in the events that led to the Sivas massacre on 2 July 1993 in Sivas, Turkey, which resulted in 37 deaths.[3]

While in England, I witnessed the effects *The Satanic Verses* had on the Muslim community, and was able to see them from both the Western and the Islamic perspectives. Rushdie is a great figure of English literature in the twentieth and twenty-first centuries. For this he was rightfully honored by Western nations, including the head of his colonial power, the Queen of England. At the same time, I understand that for Muslims it was impossible that someone should be honored for critiquing, much less mocking the Prophet.

So whereas the British saw themselves as honoring a great literary figure, Muslims saw the British queen honoring a disreputable heretic who brought shame to all Muslims.

Ironically, the Iran of Ayatollah Khomeini has become a nation in which the Christian church is growing rapidly, though Iranian officials won't admit it. One reason is that the radical Shiite Islam promoted by Khomeini and his successors is detestable to many Iranians. They live under sharia law, and in the Shiite system the Ayatollah is both the ultimate religious and political authority. The previous Iranian president, Mahmoud Ahmadinejad, was also an embarrassment to Iran given his penchant for saying ridiculous things in the international press. Well-educated Iranians, with the rich history of the Persian Empire behind them, blushed with shame at the actions of both the Ayatollah and their president. I sometimes think that God uses antiheroes like Khomeini and Ahmadinejad to spread the gospel as much as he uses Christian missionaries.

While in England in January 1997 I got a letter from my sister. This was hardly unusual, but its sad contents were. My brother Yasser died on December 24, 1996, of a heart attack. By the time I received the letter the funeral and burial services were long over. I wept and wept again, and not like a European but openly and loudly, letting my grief pour out in a long, bitter stream.

Azieza and Moustafa had decided that it would be best if I did not come to the funeral, so they sent me the letter when they knew it would be too late for me to return. It would be best for them since my presence would have brought back long-remembered shame to the family. And it would be best for me, since someone might still think they could serve Islam by killing the long-time apostate. But again, as was the case in the deaths of my cousin and my father, I saw nothing of Yasser's final parting from this world.

I felt terrible for my mother. She had buried both her husband and her son, a horrible burden. Yasser had been living with her after his divorce. He was her oldest, the successful, good son who was caring for her in her old age. I was again reminded of how close my ties to Egypt remained.

At that time I also felt—and continue to feel—bad about the fact that no others from my family have accepted Christ. Why not? Am I such a bad witness? Are the ties of Islamic society too tight for them to escape? Am I perhaps just strange, having changed my identity, and the rest of my family normal? I am hardly the only Muslim convert to ask such questions. In fact, most probably do. Christian converts from Islam are oddballs. We no longer fit in with the society we came from. Many converts are ostracized from family and society. Some converts never reveal their Christian identity and don't dare to speak of it, even with close family and friends. I continued my work with a sad heart.

Every summer I went to a Christian coffee shop in London that had been set up with the specific goal of doing evangelism among Muslims. No Muslim would be caught dead going into a church to find out about Christianity; but going to coffee shops is second nature for us Arabs. The ministry typically had a team of eight students at the shop; four would mingle with the customers on the ground floor, and four would be in prayer upstairs.

Many Muslims were curious and came in. Some grabbed a Bible and ran, but others stayed to chat and have a cup of coffee. On a number of occasions a veiled woman would sneak in and take a Bible. Then, a few days later she would be back for more materials. The student evangelists in the group were themselves Arabic speakers, so they could talk readily with the guests. The coffee shop was situated very close to a mosque, and soon news of the coffee shop's strategy came to the attention of the imam at the mosque. So each day after the afternoon prayers, the imam would come into the coffee shop. As soon as he did, every Muslim there who had been chatting about Christianity started vociferously quoting verses from the Qur'an that refuted Christianity. When the imam was confident that he had made everyone afraid to speak openly of Christianity, he left.

Okay, I understand his game, I thought to myself. The next time the imam headed toward us, I intercepted him at the door. I sat down with him and bought him a cup of coffee. Then I began to converse and debate with him about Islam and Christianity. I certainly never convinced him, but I did free the others to talk about Christ, since the imam was now so entangled in his discussion with me that he couldn't pay attention to the conversations around him.

Today there are more Muslims in England than there are Methodists. Many come from former British colonies, and some wealthy Arabs from the Gulf States also come to escape the summer heat. England is thus a mission field for Christianity in two ways: both the native British who have left Christ, and the Muslim immigrants and visitors. At the same time, the Muslims see Britain as a mission field. Though it was not my principal work, I too was able to do some evangelism while in England.

I served as a translator on occasion as well. The British have 7/7/2005 as their equivalent of 9/11/2001 in the United States. On that date bombs set by Islamic terrorists went off on three trains in London, and on a double-decker bus. Earlier, a reporter from the BBC had gone to various mosques in England and recorded what he heard. He brought some of the tapes to me for translation. What

I heard did not surprise me, but it did surprise some within the British government. In short, the imams were preaching the overthrow of the infidel nation of Great Britain. One of these prominent imams, Abu Hamza, was interviewed on Al Jazeera TV. The Arabic-speaking interviewer asked him, "Are you on welfare in England?"

"Yes," he answered.

"Do you have a British passport, and are you a subject of the Queen?" Again, his answer was yes.

"Yet you seek to overthrow the British government?"

"Yes," the imam said. "It is perfectly right for us to use the benefits of life among the infidels in order to fight the infidels."

After July 7, 2005, conversations and sermons like these got a great deal more attention.

I was later called on by a government minister to help understand what could be done about the kidnappings of some Muslim girls. The girls were from immigrant Muslim families, but they were born in England and grew up as English kids. When they got older, they liked to go out on dates like the other English kids. But they couldn't let their parents know that they had been dating English boys who weren't Muslim. When the parents inevitably found out, they were furious, feeling they had been betrayed. Often, parents like this would quickly arrange a marriage for their daughter in their country of origin—Yemen, Pakistan, Bangladesh, or any other. They would escort the daughter back and marry her off, while the girl, who was a British subject, was in her young teens. Meanwhile, her teacher would report her absent from school, and an investigation would begin. There was almost nothing that could be done. Though the girls were British subjects, they couldn't be repatriated back to England, and it was impossible to hold the parents liable for kidnapping their own daughter when there was no proof of using force.

London's Hyde Park has a wonderful tradition of open debate, which has included luminaries such as Karl Marx, George Orwell, and Vladimir Lenin in the past. In the northeast corner of the park, a debater mounts the pedestal and addresses the crowd on any subject they wish, and the crowd answers back. The speaker has to get on the official debate schedule, so the crowd knows exactly who and what to expect. Jay Smith, a Christian debater, regularly takes the podium and debates Muslim leaders.[4] Jay was raised in India, of missionary parents, and now has a PhD in Islamic studies.

When he does this, I and others would go throughout the crowd, seeing if there were any Muslims who looked interested in knowing more about Christ. If so, we spoke with them during and after the debate. But that wasn't always easy. The Muslims know Jay well, and so they have apparently hired some professional hecklers to come to the events. We recognize the hecklers, and they recognize us. Though Jay has been threatened, the vibrant tradition of free speech in English history keeps him safe.

I too used the freedom of speech guaranteed in Britain to do evangelism. One man I engaged about Islam was a Saudi Arabian who was the son of the former chief of prisons in Mecca. He told me that for every bad thing I could think of about Islam, he could do me one better. He told me horror stories about some of the things he had seen while growing up in the holy birthplace of Islam. He wanted to know the good news about Jesus, not the bad news about Islam. So he and I talked for nearly twenty-four hours over a period of four days. I told him about the first Adam, who had brought shame upon all of his children, and the second Adam, who had brought honor to his Father. I reviewed the Scriptures from

Genesis to Revelation with him, but to this day I do not know whether he accepted Christ.

Once when I was in a London park openly evangelizing among the Arabs, a man came up to me and asked in Arabic if I was a Christian. I said that I was. He asked me a couple of good questions about Christianity. I showed him what he wanted to know from Scripture, and he then asked if he could pray to become a Christian. I had never before, and have never since, seen someone who was so ready to receive Christ as he was. Clearly the Holy Spirit and perhaps other Christians had been at work in his life long before he met me.

MISUNDERSTANDINGS
in
EUROPE

Muslims know much about Christianity because the Qur'an is full of stories derived from the Bible.[1] For example, Muslims believe that Jesus was a great prophet, in fact, the second greatest, after Muhammad. They do not accept the fact, however, that God would allow his second greatest prophet to be shamefully killed. Rather, most believe that Judas was crucified, not Christ. Thus they would obviously not believe that Christ arose either.

When they begin to understand the Bible's story of the Christ who died for us because he loves us, they are either repelled or awed. "For God so loved you [Ahmed, Fatima, Mustafa, etc.] that he sent his only Son, so that if you believe in him you will not perish but have everlasting life" is indeed good news. When they see that Christians show that love to one another, the case is often sealed.

In 2005, while we were in England, a controversy erupted in a small Swiss town. The minority Muslim population there wanted to build a six-meter (twenty-foot) tall minaret on top of their Turkish/Islamic community center. Neighbors and the town planning commission rejected their request. The community center appealed the ruling all the way to the Swiss Supreme Court and was granted permission to build in 2009. The Swiss People's Party, a substantial center-right political force, campaigned against the minaret construction. They succeeded in getting one hundred thousand signatures on a constitutional initiative that would ban construction of minarets. They argued that the minarets are not necessary for the practice of Islam but are a symbol of religious and political power. They quoted from a 1997 speech by Recep Tayyip Erdoğan (later prime minister of Turkey) in which he said, "The mosques are our barracks, the domes our helmets, the minarets our bayonets, and the faithful our soldiers. This holy army guards my religion."[2] Feminists in Switzerland also objected to an Islamic symbol that celebrates the power of men over women. In 2009 the ban on minaret construction narrowly passed.[3] It is still being challenged in various cantons (especially French-speaking ones) throughout Switzerland. One of our mission's supporters was a well-connected Swiss businessman. He asked me to come to Switzerland and meet with the representative from his canton. I told him I believed that the Swiss were wise to prohibit minaret construction. A minaret is not necessary for Islamic worship, nor is it called for in the Qur'an. Minarets developed in the Islamic world when the community around a mosque grew too large to hear one man calling the faithful to prayer. They were built in order to project the sound of the call to prayer throughout the larger community.

Muslims in Switzerland today hardly need a call from a minaret to remember the hours of prayer. They could make computerized phone calls or simply look at their Swiss watches or cell phones. I suspect that the real reason the Swiss Muslims wanted to build a minaret was to symbolize their presence and power. Having the tallest edifice in a European village says something, especially if the minaret is higher than the spires of the local church.

In part, what is at play here is the Western democracies' view of religion and politics versus the Arab and Islamic view of the state and religion. As I have stated previously, Islam is one, Allah rules over all aspects of life, and the religious leaders of Islam are often de facto lawmakers of their nations. In contrast, in the West, religious and secular institutions are strictly separated. Religious affiliations are freely chosen by each person according to his or her conscience, and religious organizations function with clear limits placed on their spheres of influence. Muslims in Europe thus have wide freedoms to practice their faith, whereas non-Muslims in Islamic nations have severe restrictions placed on their freedom to worship. In all Muslim lands, Christians are prohibited from proselytizing, and even Shiite Muslim minorities in Sunni majority nations face many constraints.

The West little understands this unity of life, belief, politics, and society that is Islam. The misunderstanding goes back to the times of Muhammad himself. Muhammad is the final and true prophet of Allah in Islam; so what was revealed to him in visions is the final and complete word of God. Only Muhammad received the visions, and only the Arabic Qur'an is the true revelation of God.[4] Muhammad's visions were wide ranging and included regulations for marriage, inheritance, war, taxation, and so on. Muhammad based his authority on the visions he received, and on the divine approval he had received for his actions. In some cases the divine approval for his rulings and actions came after the fact, in later visions.[5]

Muhammad's life and teachings as recorded in the hadiths are the model for Muslims today. Where Islam rules, Islamic law must be practiced, and in such societies only Muslim men have a full set of civil rights. During his lifetime, Muhammad fought those who denied the legitimacy of his visions, and thus his power. For Islam all is one—Muhammad, the Qur'an, Islamic society, civil law, Allah, family law, and cultic practices. The contrast with the multicultural West is dramatic.

For Muslims the Qur'an cannot be changed, challenged, or even interpreted within its historical context, as is the Bible. The Qur'an is the eternally existing Word that Jibril (Gabriel) dictated to Muhammad. Professional Islamic scholars, the imams and muftis, are permitted to *apply* these words to different cases based on the consensus of previous rulings; but they are rarely permitted to interpret the Qur'an afresh. The official consensus of interpretation was fixed by the fourteenth century and is called the *ijma*; it is based on the tradition of law derived from the Qur'an and the hadiths. To live in submission to Allah is thus to be under the law of sharia, as the consensus of Islamic scholars has understood it.

Some contemporary Muslim scholars who have been trained in modern literary and historical critical methods struggle to adapt sharia to contemporary societies. One such scholar was the chief Islamist at the University of Leyden in the Netherlands. He argued that there must be contemporary interpretations of the Qur'an, and that the writings from the seventh century CE must be understood within their historical and literary context. He was declared to be a heretic, and since he was a heretic, the Islamic authorities decreed that he could not stay married to his Muslim wife. He and other progressive Muslims are often isolated or targeted in this way by the "purer" Muslims.

The worst (or most conservative) group within Islam is the Wahhabi sect. The Wahhabis are found largely in the Arabian Peninsula and are the group that Osama bin Laden came from. Saudi Arabia is the home of Mecca and Medina, and is thus considered the place where Islam is most fervently practiced. Since Saudi Arabia is fabulously wealthy, the Saudis can easily extend their influence. Imams throughout the Middle East are educated in Saudi Arabia. While I was in England, a group of British Muslims wanted to erect a new mosque. Their leader picked up the phone, called a friend in Saudi Arabia, and had a check for a million pounds sterling within the week. With that kind of financing and support, Western Muslims can isolate themselves from Western ideals and practices.

But while Muslims can freely practice their faith in the West, Westerners may no longer go openly to Islamic lands, as was true in the eighteenth and nineteenth centuries. Since the Pan-Arabic movement of the 1970s, nearly everyone associated with European colonial powers was thrown out of the Middle East. Western Christians who work in the Middle East today must have legitimate secular occupations. Some do indeed work in industry, trade, and finance, and serve as Christian witnesses wherever they are called. In Saudi Arabia, for example, churches are absolutely forbidden. The Westerners who work in the oil fields must meet for Sunday worship in the oil company's offices. Nonetheless, a few Westerners have found opportunities to speak of Christ to national leaders in Arab lands.

Relating Islam to the West and vice versa is no easy task. There are numerous misunderstandings and conflicts that make the relationship difficult, and a fourteen-hundred-year history of war and suspicion does not make things easier.

Another example of what Muslims viewed as a desecration occurred on September 30, 2005, when we lived in England. The
Danish newspaper *Jyllands-Posten* (Jutland Post) published twelve
cartoons depicting the prophet Muhammad. (Denmark has a
sizable Muslim minority.) The cartoons were published with the
explicit intention of testing whether freedom of the press in
Denmark extended to negative characterizations of Islam. Danish
cartoonists were solicited to produce their perspectives of what
Muhammad might have been like. Some declined the invitation
out of fear. All of the cartoons mocked the Prophet, and the most
provocative of them showed an Arab man with a bomb growing
out of his turban. The cartoons were subsequently published across
the globe and online, and they ignited a storm of protest from
many Muslims.

According to the Qur'an, it is horrible idolatry to compare anything to Allah or to provide any representation of him. This is the
ultimate sin of shirk. This prohibition is the reason that Islam has
no dynamic equivalent of Michelangelo's painting in the Sistine
Chapel. According to some hadiths, the Prophet also must not be
artistically depicted in any way,[6] so seeing him mocked in a Western
cartoon was scandalous. Danish embassies in Syria, Iran, and
Lebanon were fire-bombed. The cartoonists went into hiding, and
Danish goods were banned by many Muslim nations.

I grant that the cartoonists were foolish. Why did they have to
antagonize Muslims with such sacrilege? Muhammad is honored
by approximately one-fifth of the world's population, and that
population is genuinely devout in its faith. How would Christians
feel if Muslims depicted Jesus as a pedophile or a sorcerer? Nonetheless, the Danish cartoons did confirm what many Europeans

suspected: when it comes to freedom of speech and the press in Europe, Islam is a formidable and dangerous exception.

Muslims cannot comprehend how someone can be permitted to blaspheme against Islam. In their home countries, it would never happen. I once was at the home of an Arab Muslim friend in London. He and I had talked about religion on a couple of occasions. His brother came over, and we continued our conversation. His brother got extremely upset that we could openly raise questions about Islam. He knew, however, that in England there was nothing he could do about it. Nonetheless, he went out into the street and shouted the Shahada at the top of his voice so that the whole Arab neighborhood could hear him. He wanted to prove to all within shouting distance that, unlike his brother, he was still a good Muslim.

The violence seen in these responses to blasphemy has a long history. When the Muslim Arabs took over neighboring peoples in the seventh century and beyond, they offered the conquered peoples three options: convert to Islam, accept dhimmitude, or face continued war. Dhimmitude is obviously the least well known and understood of the three options, but it likely has the longest-lasting influence.[7] To be a dhim, you first had to be one of the conquered "People of the Book" (that is, a Christian or Jew). A dhim who lived in a Muslim-controlled land was required to make a covenant of loyalty to its Muslim ruler and pay a special tax, called the *jizya*. This tax could be equal to as much as one fourth of the annual earnings for an average worker, and it became a major source of income for many Muslim rulers. The jizya is not the same as the Muslim tithe (zakat). The zakat is one of the five pillars of Islam and is equivalent to about one tenth of a years' labor; its revenues were used to aid poor Muslims. But the jizya was more than a tax.

Today it would be called more of a "tribute" or even "protection money." If the dhimmi failed to pay the jizya, they would be considered to be in rebellion and could be killed as enemies. In other words, the payment of jizya was a dhim's way of staying alive as a religious minority in an Islamic land.

There was a ceremony that symbolized this process of submission. The dhim would not be permitted to simply show up at the ancient tax office and write out his annual jizya check. Dhimmi would have to personally appear in a public arena in which the Muslim overlords could literally look down on them. The hands of the lords would be at least at the level of the heads of the dhimmi, suggesting that they were at a point in which they could easily execute them with a sword. Upon payment, each dhim was sometimes beaten and was always struck with a fist across the back of the neck, symbolizing decapitation by sword.[8] The message was very clear: by making this payment you escape death.

Dhimmitude appears to be resurfacing in countries where sharia law is in effect. There are reports that it may be in play in Muslim-ruled Malaysia and in conservative villages in Egypt and elsewhere. It also has been practiced by the Islamic State (ISIS) in Syria and Iraq. Given international law and the United Nations Declaration on Human Rights, dhimmitude clearly cannot be openly espoused or practiced, but its fourteen-hundred-year-old tradition leaves deep memories in Muslim nations.

It is sometimes hard for Westerners to believe that apostasy and blasphemy laws or practices such as dhimmitude still exist in the twenty-first century. One Syrian English scholar of comparative religions went to Egypt to investigate reports of the persecution of Christians. He apparently thought he would be welcomed into the offices of the secret police and they would hand him files marked

"Christian Persecution Plan" or perhaps "Names and Dates of our Christian Victims." When he did not find such files, he went back to England and blithely reported that there is no persecution of Christians in Egypt. Such is the naiveté of the West.

In comparison to Islam, the origins of Christianity are quite different. When Christianity began, it was a tiny sect coming out of a small religion (Judaism) in a remote corner of the vast Roman Empire. Therefore, new Christian believers in Palestine, the lands around the Aegean Sea, contemporaneous Turkey, Egypt, Syria, and so forth had to adapt to the laws and customs of the local peoples. They did not establish a Christian state or law, but lived under the Roman Empire and its law. Nearly three centuries elapsed before Constantine emerged and there was concord between Christianity and the state (313 CE). Before then, early Christians were subject to persecution at local and occasionally empire-wide levels.

In contrast, Islam began as a political-religious movement and quickly developed into an empire. At the time of Muhammad, the Christian Byzantine Empire, centered in Constantinople, was corrupt and splintered by heresies. The superficially Christian Persian Empire was also weakened by theological conflict. Byzantium and Persia were often at war with each other, and into this context Islam was born. By the time the Prophet died in 632 CE, he had conquered much of the enormous Arabian Peninsula. (The Arabian Peninsula is approximately the size of all of Western Europe, one-third the size of the continental United States.) His immediate successor, Abu Bakr (632–634), conquered the remainder of the Arabian Peninsula in just two years before he was killed. Umar (634–644) extended Islam into contemporary Iraq, Syria, Jordan, and Eastern Egypt. Uthman and Ali (644–661) conquered the remainder of Egypt, plus the areas of modern Libya, Persia, Iran, Pakistan, Afghanistan, Armenia, Azerbaijan, and Eastern Turkey. From their base in Damascus, the Umayyads (661–750) finished the conquest of all of North Africa, took Spain, Portugal, Sicily, Corsica, and Sardinia in the West, and extended the empire into the western frontiers of contemporary India and China. Thus, in little over a hundred years from the death of the Prophet, Muslims ruled over a larger empire than had the Persians, Greeks, or Romans before them.

Spain itself was controlled by the Muslims for over seven hundred years (711–1492). Islam spread through Eastern Europe into Bulgaria, Romania, Serbia, Moldavia, and even Austria under the Ottoman Turks. So when Islam interacts with Europe today, memories of its earlier history are evident, if submerged. Whereas Muslims know that dhimmitude is now politically impossible, they see its practice as the high watermark of Islam's Golden Age.

Note that the lands that the first four "Rightly Guided Caliphs" conquered were majority Christian nations.[9] The Eastern Orthodox Churches extended throughout North Africa into contemporary Syria, Jordan, Turkey, Armenia, Iraq, and so on. These churches began in apostolic times and had grown in that region for over five hundred years prior to the birth of Muhammad. I grant that Christianity may have been the official religion of the state rather than the religion of the people's hearts in some of these places; nonetheless, it was hardly a religious vacuum into which Islam entered after the death of the Prophet. In a sense, the conquest of Islam into Byzantium was a Muslim Crusade, at least five hundred years before the more well-known Christian Crusades.

Muslims are loath to acknowledge that they ever wage anything but defensive wars. They describe the initial conquest as the "opening," which Allah gave them to spread Islam. Any nation or group who opposes Islam is the one who is offensive; Muslims are simply defending the faith. Everywhere they conquered, they established Islamic law (sharia) and created an Islamic state ruled by caliphs. The law, derived from the visions and life of Muhammad, became the standard for long-standing civilizations that stretched from Cairo to Cordoba, and from Baghdad to Kabul. The rule of Islam did look different from one culture to another, but the unity of Islam was impregnable. As always, it was one God, one prophet, one rule. This condition, in which Islam was dominant, is seen by Muslims as the ideal. It is thus a source of great annoyance that the "Christian" West has overtaken them in technology and education, as well as in economic, political, and military power.

Today, Islam is growing in Europe, due to immigration and high birth rates. Some Eastern European countries, such as Serbia, have held large populations of Muslims for centuries. A leading Turkish imam said, "We will bury you with our high birth rate." In France there are 3.5 million Muslims, and they account for 6 percent of its population; Germany has four million Muslims, or 4 percent of its population; a little under a million in the Netherlands, or 5.7 percent of its population, and so forth.[10] As the Muslim populations grow, so does the problem of incorporating a monotheistic sociopolitical system into a pluralistic society.

When Muslim converts to Christianity get into Europe from Arab lands, they are rarely if ever granted religious asylum. Even though the law of apostasy reigns throughout most Muslim lands, Western governments rarely acknowledge that Christians there are threatened. Western nations note that the general assembly of the United Nations, which includes Muslims countries, approved the Declaration on Human Rights, and in that declaration freedoms of religion and conscience are guaranteed. But many Islamic nations, such as Saudi Arabia, Pakistan, and (now Northern) Sudan have protested that the UN declaration represents only a Western view of rights. They argue that even these basic rights must be subject to interpretation under sharia law. In effect, this vacates the Declaration on Human Rights and replaces it with sharia law.

At the same time, Islamic leaders themselves struggle to understand their role as a minority religion in the West. They have no theoretical system for living as a minority in a non-Muslim land. Since their history is one of conquest by sword, conversion, or trade, the lands they conquered were soon majority Muslim. That was when and where they knew how to live. But when they are the minority, the Qur'an and many traditions from the hadiths create conflict for them. To be good Muslims, they should follow sharia law. Some of the sharia law that relates to family and ritual practices can be followed while living in the West, but much cannot. Many Western Muslims are at a loss as to what to do. If they give up the Muslim customs and law, they feel as if they are giving up their very identity. But they cannot be complete Muslims in a non-Muslim land.

In England, polygamy illustrates this problem. In Islam, a man is permitted to have up to four wives at a time. In Britain, one is standard. But Muslims argue that polygamy is a tenet of their faith, and they should be allowed the free exercise of their faith. It's a nice conundrum. An Afghan convert in England once asked me, "As a Muslim, I beat my wife five times a day. Now that I am a Christian, how often should I beat her?" How do you reconcile these religious-cultural practices of Islam with the laws and customs of the West?

Recently, former British prime minister David Cameron has shown a clearer understanding than most of the difficulty of integrating Islam into modern Europe. He speaks about mosques and Islamic groups in England:

Let's properly judge these organisations: Do they believe in universal human rights—including for women and people of other faiths? Do they believe in equality of all before the law? Do they believe in democracy and the right of people to elect their own government? Do they encourage integration or separatism? These are the sorts of questions we need to ask. Fail these tests and the presumption should be not to engage with such organizations.[11]

In 1949, Muslim Pakistan split from Hindu India because the two faiths could not be reconciled. It remains to be seen how Europe will accommodate and reconcile itself to the increasing Muslim population in its midst.

Many Arabs in Europe have become Christian. But Europe, like the Middle East, provides its own set of challenges for them. On the one hand, Muslim converts typically live in Arab or Turkish enclaves, so new converts there may face the same difficulties in Europe that they did in the Middle East. On the other hand, the broader Western society they are a part of is predominantly secular, so new Christian believers are out of place there as well. In fact, given the preponderance of secularity in Europe, it is rare that Muslim converts can find a European church in which they will feel welcomed, so Christian Arabs in Europe are often isolated, with few models for their faith.

One Christian group that has been successful in keeping Muslim converts in the church is called the Oasis. The Oasis recognizes that the church is both a social and a spiritual entity. They serve ethnic food, perform worship services in the native languages, and respect the validity of the Middle Eastern cultures for new Christians. I know that the ideal would be to have believers from all ethnic groups together as a representation of God's diverse family, but for new converts from Islam I think that may be impossible. They need some parts of their identity to hold on to.

Some Muslim converts have moved from Christianity on to secularism or religious pluralism. One woman I was instrumental in helping get from the Middle East to Europe married a German pastor. When I called her later to see if she could help with a Christian project, she declined. She said that she was going to pursue a doctorate in comparative religious studies in order to show that Islam and Christianity were equally valid ways to know God.

The well-known author of *Infidel*, Ayaan Hirsi Ali, has a similar story. She was raised as a Muslim in Somalia, Kenya, and Saudi Arabia. After many years in Europe she found she could no longer accept a God like Allah and a prophet like Muhammad, especially given their extravagant endorsements of misogyny. In her case, the belief that "there is one God Allah, and Muhammad is his prophet," evolved into "I believe there is neither God nor prophet."[12] A secularized person is often more difficult to reach for Christ than is a Muslim. Muslims readily agree that there is a God and that the material world is not all there is to life. The secularist, on the other hand, is not convinced of the existence of a God or an afterlife, and thinks they know enough about religion to dismiss it. Since most Europeans are secular, many Muslim converts have problems finding fellow Christian believers with whom they can pray and worship.

Secular Europe is not always amenable to Christian evangelism of Muslims either. An Arab woman convert in the Netherlands led her husband to Christ. They together led another woman to Christ. That woman's Muslim husband then stabbed the Christian husband. Though he was arrested, the attitude of the Dutch authorities seemed to be, "That will teach you to proselytize." In England an evangelist to Muslims was set on fire with kerosene. The police did little to find the perpetrator. Many Western Europeans would like to pretend that there really aren't millions of Muslims in their midst. Or if they acknowledge that there are Muslims present, they pretend that there is really no difference between them and the Westerners.

Today there are more Muslims in France than there are evangelical Christians. We estimate that in 2010 about fifteen thousand of these French Muslims have converted to Christ. Twenty years ago we knew of only about ten Muslim converts to Christianity in all of France. Clearly the Muslims in Europe are a field ready for harvest.

CHAPTER TEN

CHRISTIANS
in
EGYPT

As my sister knows, it can be difficult to be a Muslim woman. As I know from experience, it can also be difficult and even deadly to be a Christian or a Jew in Muslim countries. These difficult relationships have a long history.

"People of the Book" is the name Muslims give to Jews and Christians. Jews have the book of the Law as their Holy Scripture, and Christians have the gospel as theirs. Muslims accept both of these testaments of Scripture, but see the revelation given to Muhammad in the Qur'an as the final and true revelation of God.

How this works out in practice is sometimes funny and sometimes dangerous. For example, in grade school we performed many little plays, one of which was about the Palestinians and the Israelis. I was given the role of Moshe Dayan, so I got to wear an eye patch. The Israelis, of course, were not liked, especially Moshe. In our play, the Palestinians came in and killed all the Israelis, including Moshe.

For years after that my classmates still teasingly called me Moshe. I didn't appreciate it.

Arab children are taught to hate the Israelis from an early age. In the newspapers and other media, Jews are depicted as misers, cheats, and liars. They are remembered as the infidels who first opposed the prophet Muhammad. They are the ones we refer to when we recite the first chapter of the Qur'an: "Guide us to the straight path—the path of those upon whom You have bestowed favor, not of those who have evoked [Your] anger or of those who are astray."

Arab histories of the Middle East often eliminate or minimize the contributions of the Jews. For example, Egyptian history is often told as if there were never any Jews in Egypt, though there were Jews in Egypt long before Muslims were. Until quite recently there were major synagogues and large Jewish-owned businesses in Cairo that were well recognized. Long before they have ever met an Israeli, most Egyptians will have developed a strong antipathy toward them.[1]

I have been to Palestine no fewer than ten times in recent years. I go sometimes to teach at Bethlehem Bible College, to speak at conferences, or simply to uphold the struggling Arab Christians who are there. If I visit Muslim converts in Palestine, I do not openly declare myself to be a Christian evangelist, since many of these converts prefer to keep their beliefs private. Like Muslim converts elsewhere, publicly declaring their faith could result in discrimination from family, community, or government.

Egypt is near the center of all three of the Abrahamic religions' histories. Archaeological records show that the civilization of the Nile has flourished at least four thousand years before Christ. Southern Egypt is called the Upper Nile, which flows into the Lower Nile, eventually pouring into the Mediterranean.

Contemporary Egypt is approximately one and a half times the size of Texas, and ancient Egypt was larger still, extending into contemporary Sudan, Libya, and Israel. This is the ancient civilization out of which Judaism and Christianity were born, but which Islam has ruled for the last fourteen hundred years.

As early as a decade after the resurrection of Christ, the apostle Mark is believed to have evangelized Egypt. In fact, the Coptic Church maintains a bishopric believed to be directly descended from him, called the Basilica of St. Mark. The term *Coptic* is a transliteration of the word *Egyptian* in Greek. When Egypt was ruled by the successors of Alexander the Great, they gave the Egyptians this name.[2] Copts are those who have remained Christian even after the Muslim conquest, and they are proud to be one of the oldest Christian traditions in the world. They take special pride in the Gospel story in which the holy family fled from Herod to safety in Egypt.

Early Coptic Christianity was threatened by the polytheism of its neighboring tribes as well as the philosophies of the Greco-Roman world. To defend itself intellectually, Egyptian Christians established a superb catechetical university in Alexandria, where students from around the Mediterranean world studied Christian theology. As one of the Eastern Churches, its language of scholarship was Greek, not Latin.

Alexandria was one of the three greatest centers of the Christian faith in the first five centuries of Christianity. (The others were Rome and Syrian Antioch.) Church fathers such as Origen, Clement, and Athanasius were from what is now Egypt, as was the heretic Arius. Christ had more than a foothold in North Africa. In fact, for over five hundred years Christianity was the majority religion of the region.

The desert fathers, those Christian hermits and monks who established the pattern for all future monastic movements, were also Egyptian. As early as 270 CE, the Egyptian Saint Anthony was able to commit his sister to what would now be called a convent. In 305 CE Anthony moved most of the Egyptian monasteries from the cities into the wilderness, so they could better focus on spiritual things. By the fourth century CE it was said that almost every Egyptian town had a monastery nearby.

The Christian church in Egypt suffered horribly under the persecutions of Roman emperors Nero, Decius, and Diocletian. Diocletian alone killed so many Christians in Egypt in 284 CE that the Coptic calendar takes its start from that "Year of the Martyrs." Copts have been a part of Egypt since the first century of Christianity, but since the expansion of Islam they have become an oppressed minority. They currently number about 10 to 12 percent of the Egyptian population and face the demolition of their churches and persecution by radical Islamic groups such as the Muslim Brotherhood and the Islamic State. Usually, Coptic babies are tattooed with a little cross on their wrists. The tattoo remains with them for life, so when they are in a bus or a train and are holding a rail, their wrist tattoos can be seen.

Muhammad was born in Mecca, on the western edge of Arabian Peninsula, in approximately 570 CE. He had his first vision as a prophet in 610, later called the "Night of Power." He left Mecca under pressure from the Meccans, who did not accept his visions of God or his pretensions to political power. He and his followers made their famous journey to Medina in 622. Known as the Hegira, this story is as well known among Muslim children as the story of Jesus' birth in a manger in Bethlehem is among Christians. The Hegira is year zero in the Islamic calendar; thus

Muslims are now living in the fourteen hundreds. By the time he died in 632 CE, Muhammad was the ruler of virtually the entire Arabian Peninsula, and he had established the world's third and last Abrahamic religion.

Muhammad initially expected the Jews and Christians to accept him as the last of the prophets. In fact, he is still known by Muslims as "the Seal of the Prophets," or the one who closes the period of God's revelation. As he came into contact with more Jews in Medina, however, he realized that many of them would never accept him. He broke off relations with the Jews and demonstrated the break by changing the direction he bowed during his daily prayers, from Jerusalem to Mecca (sura 2:144).

After the death of Muhammad, Islam rapidly moved west and northward from its home in the Arabian Peninsula. When the Arab Muslims arrived in Egypt they found a highly developed civilization, far more advanced than that of the Arab invaders themselves. From 639 to 642, Muhammad's followers laid siege to and conquered the largely Christian city of Alexandria. In the period of Islam's Golden Age (750–1258), universities flourished and the sciences made great advances. The mathematical genius of the Arabs was seen in the development of algebra, and philosophy from ancient Greece served as a basis for Islamic scholars. Islam expanded by trade, conquest, and intellectual dominance.

Contemporary Egyptians are the descendants of those Arab conquerors and native Egyptians. Egyptians today are almost exclusively Sunni Muslim, as are about 85 percent of the Muslims in the world today. The remaining 15 percent are Shiite, found largely in Iran and southern Iraq. *Sunna* means "normative path" or "pattern of the Prophet," and entails obedience to the Qur'an and respect for the wisdom and life of the Prophet. Reports of the

Prophet's sayings and life are called hadiths, biographical collections of Muhammad's life and words. Within Sunni Islam there are four main schools of law. The vast majority of Egyptians, including my family, are of the Hanafi school, a mainline Muslim branch of law.

Egypt has been under the rule of other empires since the invasion of the Persians in 343 BCE. The Persians, as well as Greeks, Romans, Byzantines, Arabs, Ottoman Turks, and later the French and the English, have all taken Egypt as their colony. But since 642 CE, Egypt has been Islamic in culture and religion.

Copts have always been present as a significant minority in Egypt, though often an oppressed one. I was even one of their oppressors. When I was in grade school, a Coptic boy was in my class. I still remember his name, Gad. I persecuted that poor child. My classmates and I pestered and harassed him day after day. We called him the typical names we reserved for Christians—"Dog of the Cross," "Blue Bones," "Infidel." One time, we even beat him up and demanded that he say the Shahada. And he did—in order to avoid another beating. But I have no illusions that we made him a Muslim convert that day, and remembering the way I treated him still brings me shame.

In Muslim Egypt there was once a Christian monastic order. The Muslim caliph ruling at the time decided to harass them by making them wear enormous crosses around their necks. The monks wearing those heavy crosses became so stooped over from the weight of the cross that their upper backbones protruded, causing black and blue marks along their spines. That's why we Muslims called the Coptic Christians "Blue Bones" when we were kids. Another slur the Muslims call the Copts is "Oiler" or "Oily," based on the Copts' use of oils for anointing and healing. And then there is always "Dog of the Cross," which unites two things despised in Islam—dogs and the cross.

Nevertheless, many Copts were successful under Muslim rule. They knew that they needed to develop movable assets, since they could be expelled from Egypt at any time. So they typically did not invest in real estate, for example, but instead in gems. They became highly educated and skilled, again knowing that they could take their skills and professions with them if forced to emigrate. Many rose to high positions in government and business. But those achievements could be turned against them. For example, one contemporary Copt managed to achieve the highest rank at the Police Academy Hospital in Cairo, and powerful Muslim politicians took exception to that. As a result, they promoted my brother, the next highest Muslim official, to that position.

In my lifetime, things have gotten worse for Copts in Egypt. Anwar Sadat Islamicized Egypt and amended the constitution to say that no law in Egypt could contradict sharia law. He also promoted Islam by establishing a strictly Islamic university to compete with the University of Cairo. Since the Islamic university required one year of religious (Islamic) studies, no Christians could possibly attend. More recently the Muslim Brotherhood has gained and then lost power.

One example of the bad news that occurs when the Islamists gain control in Egypt is that the legal age of marriage for girls is brought down to the age of nine, which was the age of Muhammad's youngest spouse, Aisha. Thus, marriage at that age is acceptable within sharia law.

Policies such as this send chills down the spines of not only Egyptian Christians but Westerners in general. May God protect Coptic Christians and encourage them to stand strong in their faith.

CHAPTER ELEVEN

ISRAEL
and the
MUSLIMS

Alongside the Christian and Muslim history of Egypt runs that of Israel, both ancient and modern. To say that Israel and Egypt have a long and complicated past is to put it mildly. According to the book of Exodus, the story of Israel itself begins in Egypt. It is clear from the biblical history of Israel that there are many parallels between it and Egyptian religion and society. For example, ancient Egyptian religion had long acknowledged the death and resurrection of a god—the sun god—as well as a day of judgment and a paradise for believers. Moses was raised as a prince in Egypt, and the two sons of Joseph (Ephraim and Manasseh) had an Egyptian mother. Ancient Israel was born out of Egypt, and you might say that modern-day Israel was born out of Egypt as well.

This is because Egypt, Syria, and other nations of the Middle East created the conditions that led to the establishment of the modern state of Israel. At the time of Christ, Philo of Alexandria reports that there were approximately one million Jews in Egypt, or nearly one-eighth of the Egyptian population.[1] Many Jews migrated to Egypt at the time of the Babylonian exile, and developed a thriving economic and intellectual society in Egypt (see Jeremiah 41:16–42:22). Their history under the Muslim Arabs was up and down: sometimes they enjoyed relative peace and prosperity, and other times they endured exorbitant taxation and persecution. By 1917, the number of Jews in Egypt was down to about sixty thousand.[2] And in 1956, to promote his pan-Arab program, Nasser expelled most of the Jews from Egypt, where they had lived for hundreds of years. They had nowhere to go. They were refugees in need of a homeland. This need, combined with the horrors of the Holocaust, created the political conditions that brought about the modern state of Israel.

To create the state of Israel, the Israelis had to forcibly take the land from the Palestinians. Under the leadership of David Ben-Gurion and Golda Meir, the Israelis killed some and removed many of the men, women, and children from the land they had lived and toiled on for centuries. The Israeli government set up a working group called "The Committee on Population Transfer," dedicated to the removal of the Palestinians.[3] After taking power in 1948, the Israeli government emptied and destroyed 400 Palestinian villages and evicted over 100,000 Palestinians.[4] A considerable number of these Palestinians were Christian. In fact, one of the most ancient Christian traditions, the Maronites (named after St. Maron), is Palestinian.

The history of this animosity among the "People of the Book" is lengthy. The principal source of this conflict is the long-standing dispute over Jerusalem. By the time of Muhammad, the temple of

Jerusalem had been built and destroyed two times. Solomon's temple was destroyed by the Babylonians in 587 BCE, and Herod's temple by the Romans in 70 CE. The site of the temple remained well known. Near that same site, in about 530 CE, the Christian emperor in Constantinople, Justinian, built the Church of Our Lady. In 619, Muhammad experienced his amazing Night Journey from Mecca to Jerusalem on a speedy flying mule.[5] In that vision, Muhammad prayed at a rock near the ancient site of the temple. He then ascended through the seven heavens and was introduced to previous prophets of Allah, whom he led in prayer. He spoke with Allah, and they discussed how often a Muslim must pray. He saw residents of both heaven and hell and then returned to Mecca. His immediate successor Umar built a rough structure on the site, but then in 705 CE Abd al-Malik built the al-Aqsa Mosque on this very site in Jerusalem to commemorate Muhammad's Night Journey. This place, now called the Dome of the Rock, is considered the third most holy place in Islam by Sunni Muslims. This site—indeed, Jerusalem itself—has been fought over for hundreds of years and is sacred to Judaism, Islam, and some Christians. I say "some Christians" because I personally cannot justify devotion to any particular historical site.

In Islam this place, Mecca, and other locales are considered holy. For Jews, the site of the temple and the entire land of Israel is considered holy, yielding the common name—the Holy Land. But Jesus denied that one place was more holy than another. He told the Samaritan woman at the well that his followers would worship in neither Jerusalem nor Samaria, but "in the Spirit and in truth" (John 4:24). Jesus also said, "My kingdom is not of this world" (John 18:36). St. Paul later described the church as holy, clearly meaning that the *people* who make up the church are holy, not a building.

I think that accepting the Christian view that believers rather than places are holy may be the only remedy for the conflict over Jerusalem. I realize this is but a dream, but were Christians in control of Jerusalem, they should not be nearly so zealous about controlling or confiscating land, since it is not the land that produces faith. On the other hand Muslims, as well as Zionists, believe that control of the land is a necessary part of their faith. And in this way, they contradict Jesus by arguing that their kingdom must indeed be part of this world.

Unfortunately, many Christian evangelicals in the United States do not see Jerusalem and Zionism in this way. For them, the contemporary state of Israel equals the people of God, and even Arab Christians living in Palestine are its enemies. They fail to distinguish between an ancient people and a modern state, and they see support for the modern state of Israel as equivalent to support for the ancient people of God. Viewed in this way, the modern state of Israel has received exuberant support in its oppression of the Palestinians from powerful American evangelicals. Some have used their financial and media empires to help sustain the empire of Israel. They finance the return of Jews from Russia, the Middle East, the United States, and elsewhere in order to repopulate modern Israel, with the hope of bringing about the return of the Messiah.

A Christian evangelical speaker at one seminar I attended in Palestine spoke to his largely Arab audience about the role of Israel in the future. He argued that the Palestinians had fallen from God's grace because of their opposition to Israel. As a result, they should have no place in modern Israel—or the future heavenly Jerusalem. A fellow Christian Egyptian at the seminar walked out, and I'm sure others felt the same way.

In a way, Zionists are similar to Muslim jihadists. Both believe that their God has promised them a land. Both believe that they have a right to that territory. Both claim Abraham as their ancestor. Both believe that God will return once they have purified that land, and both are willing to use violence to gain the territory they believe is theirs. Many jihadists would like to destroy Israel altogether; Zionists who are willing to destroy Palestine are dangerously close to them politically.

The basis of the Christian Zionist belief is that the promises made to Abraham in Genesis 15:18 and 17:8 are still literally valid and applicable in contemporary Palestine.

On that day the LORD made a covenant with Abram and said, "To your descendants I give this land, from the Wadi of Egypt to the great river, the Euphrates." (Genesis 15:18)

The whole land of Canaan, where you now reside as a foreigner, I will give as an everlasting possession to you and your descendants after you; and I will be their God. (Genesis 17:8)

Interestingly, the first enunciation of the Abrahamic covenant, in Genesis 12, does not promise land at all; rather, it merely promises Abram a great name and blessing:

I will make you into a great nation,
    and I will bless you;
I will make your name great,
    and you will be a blessing.
I will bless those who bless you,
    and whoever curses you I will curse;
and all peoples on earth
    will be blessed through you. (Genesis 12:2-3)

Notice that in this first passage of the promise, God's goal is that Abram would be a blessing to the nations—not their conqueror.

Insisting that these promises of the land of Palestine made to Abraham are literally true today, however, ignores the nearly four thousand years of subsequent history, not the least important of which includes the New Testament period. It ignores the progressive nature of biblical revelation in which the fulfillment of Old Testament promises occurs in new and surprising ways in the New Testament. In the Old Testament period the Israelites were exiled from Palestine many times. The Assyrians and Babylonians sent the Israelites into exile, and the Egyptians, Syrians, Greeks, and Romans overran and sometimes ruled over parts of its territory. The reason for their exiles is clearly stated by the prophets: they were being punished for their wickedness. In one case, the Bible says that they were so wicked that God could not even stand to live together with them in the Promised Land (see 2 Kings 17:20). The Israelites failed to keep the covenant, so the land, which was given to them as a covenant blessing, was taken from them as a covenantal curse. The Israelites never held a title to the land; it was always to be understood as a gift from God. As Leviticus 25:23 reads, "The land must not be sold permanently, because the land is mine and you reside in my land as foreigners and strangers." Holding the land required fidelity to the giver of the land and to his covenant law.

The land was given to God's people in order that they might have a place to show forth God's justice. But it was always a provisional gift, requiring Israel to do justice in that very place.[6] The fact that Israel was to be a model of justice goes back to God's relationship with the father of Israel (Abraham) himself. When about to punish Sodom, God says,

Shall I hide from Abraham what I am about to do? Abraham will surely become a great and powerful nation, and all nations on earth will be blessed through him. For I have chosen him, so that he will direct his children and his household after him to keep the way of the LORD by doing what is right and just, so that the LORD will bring about for Abraham what he has promised him. (Genesis 18:17-19)

Justice and promise have always been unbreakable chain links in the Old Testament, tied together in covenant. The father of the covenant, Abraham, is set before the nations as a model of justice. But when Abraham's children became models of injustice, the covenant promises, including that of the land, are nullified. In Deuteronomy 28, Moses says,

If you do not obey the LORD your God and do not carefully follow all his commands and decrees I am giving you today, all these curses will come on you and overtake you. (v. 15)

The LORD will drive you and the king you set over you to a nation unknown to you or your ancestors. (v. 36)

The foreigners who reside among you will rise above you higher and higher, but you will sink lower and lower. They will lend to you, but you will not lend to them. They will be the head, but you will be the tail. (vv. 43-44)

The LORD will scatter you among all nations, from one end of the earth to the other. (v. 64)

Covenant curses such as these were enacted throughout Israel's history when Israel acted unjustly.

When Jesus lived in Israel, the land he walked on was not his own; it was under the control of Rome. The Zealots of his day were committed to retaking the land from Rome through violent revolution. Jesus forcefully rejected this Zionistic plan on many occasions.[7] It was never Jesus' mission to reestablish a Davidic state whose borders ran from Egypt to Syria. Rather, it was his mission to establish the rule of the kingdom of God, which, he said, is "not of this world." As he told Peter on the Mount of Olives, when the latter pressed him to use violence to establish his rule, "Do you think I cannot call on my Father, and he will at once put at my disposal more than twelve legions of angels?" (Matthew 26:53).

The belief that the state of Israel must be reestablished before the messianic age can come ignores the fact that the Messiah himself did not once claim that the Jews needed to return to Israel before his second coming. In fact, Jesus condemned those who wished to establish an earthly and political kingdom based on Jewish identity. Instead, he made the kingdom of God available to all who would repent and receive baptism. After Jesus' resurrection, his disciples asked, "Are you at this time going to restore the kingdom of Israel?" He answered, "It is not for you to know the times or dates the Father has set by his own authority. But you will receive power when the Holy Spirit comes on you; and you will be my witnesses in Jerusalem, and in all Judea and Samaria, and to the ends of the earth" (Acts 1:6-8).

Jesus' statement is not merely an expression of ignorance about the date of the second coming. It is a statement about salvation and the land as well. Jesus answers the disciples' question in the negative. He in effect says, "No, I am not going to restore the kingdom of Israel as a political entity at this time or any other. Rather, my people will be those on whom I pour out my Spirit. And they will come from Judea and Samaria, to be sure, but that is just the start. On the basis of the Spirit's witness among you, my kingdom will be peopled from the whole world." The Jews present at Pentecost were certainly the people on whom God first poured out his Spirit, but that primacy in order in no way requires the establishment of a Zionist state.

The notion that New Testament Christians must come to Jerusalem or that Jews must again become part of Israel is another belief not present in Scripture. The story of Pentecost shows that from its inception the church was an international institution that has no sacred space beyond itself. The idea that new Christians needed to take on Jewish identity was forcefully refuted by St. Paul in letters to both the Romans and the Galatians. In these letters Paul clearly established the fact that the sons and daughters of Abraham are not those who share in the genetics or the native land of Abraham, but in his faith alone. Romans 4:9-17 tells the story. Verse 17 says, "As it is written 'I have made you a father of many nations.' He is our father in the sight of God, in whom he believed—the God who gives life to the dead and calls into being things that were not."

John the Baptist also refers to the diminished importance of Jewish identity: "Do not think you can say to yourselves, 'We have Abraham as our father.' I tell you that out of these stones God can raise up children for Abraham" (Matthew 3:9).

Jesus did not attempt to overthrow the Roman Empire of his day, but contemporary Zionists, both Jewish and Christian, want to overthrow Palestinians and Arabs, many of whom are Christian, in order to support their expansionist agenda for the state of Israel. But Christianity is not a faith in the expansion of the Israeli state; it is faith that *Adonai* (the Lord) rewards all those who love him. And those he loves he will bless with a new city made without hands, whose maker and founder is never to be the prime minister of Israel, but God himself.

In short, the kingdom of God is not built around territory but on justice. God gave his covenant people the land as a gift, in order that they might show forth and shout out God's justice. But when they themselves were unjust, the gift of the land was rescinded. Christ reestablished God's justice and showed all people how to be made just through faith in him. Never did Jesus claim that justice or justification required a physical presence in the territory of Palestine—or a genetic connection to Abraham.

Zionism is often an enormous hindrance to the spread of the gospel among Arab Muslims. Most Arabs see Americans, and especially evangelical Americans, as supporters of Zionism. If Christian Zionism were true, a new Christian convert from an Arab-Muslim background would have to become part of a political-social system that has killed and exiled both Muslims and Christians. Such a person would have to accept the forced migrations of the Palestinians as part of God's plan for the church, and believe that the injustices of the Israeli state are the necessary and proper prelude to the return of the Messiah. Given all this, Christian Zionism has become an enormous barrier to Christian mission among Arabs today.

I saw this problem firsthand when I worked with a young Christian woman in Palestine. She held all these contradictions: Am I an Arab, a Christian, a Jew? How must I relate to the state of Israel and to the Jews? If she believed some of the evangelical preachers mentioned previously, she would have to accept that she had been saved through the Jewish people and the Israeli state. She would have to work for the establishment of Israel as a purely Jewish entity that would bring about the second coming of the Messiah. I assured her that this was not correct. God called and loved her as an Arab woman, who now, in Christ, did not need to go through Israel or Christian men in order to have a fully satisfying relationship with God.

On one of my trips to Israel, I visited a struggling church. Its members were poor Arab Christians. They were under fire from both the Israelis and their neighboring Muslims—being neither fish nor fowl, they were rejected by the Muslims for converting to Christianity and rejected by the Israelis because they were Arabs.

On another trip to Palestine, I visited a Palestinian convert in the Gaza Strip who was raised in the United States and was teaching English in Palestine and also running a ministry for handicapped children. While walking from our hotel to the university, we got word from one of his students: "Run! Hamas has targeted you for kidnapping."[8] We did run. Had the call come one minute later, we would have been captured. I was not the target, but they would have gladly grabbed me as a bonus, demanding a ransom for me as well. In Palestine, religious and political differences can cost you your life.

Some children in Palestine are taught to prepare themselves to die in support of their country. They sing an Arabic rhyme: "By the millions, by the millions, we will die for Palestine."[9] My friend who works with handicapped children is also a fine musician. He was raised in Houston by a Palestinian father and a North American mother, and so learned Arabic as a child. He taught these children Christian songs, including "Jesus Loves Me." They were taken aback when they learned that someone gave his life for them and wasn't asking them to give their lives for him. At one of his concerts someone (likely from Hamas) shot through his guitar while he was playing it. The musician was later expelled from Palestine by the Israelis. I don't know what pretext they gave, but the truth is that they couldn't stand having an American Palestinian living in the Gaza Strip who loved the Palestinians and was loved by them.

The two main political parties in Palestine are Fatah and Hamas. Fatah is more amenable to Israel and the West, but they are also more crooked. They stole on a grand scale from the relief funds that came to them from the West, building villas for themselves that overlook the Mediterranean. Hamas, on the other hand, is more honest with the money, and it supported the poor of Palestine even while out of power. Hamas won the election in Palestine in 2006. They are extremely opposed to the state of Israel and anti-Western in general. Since they are related to Shiite Iran they are also anathema to Sunni Saudi Arabia and the majority of Sunni Arabs.

One young man whose father was a Hamas leader became a Christian. He stayed in Palestine for some time afterward, but he finally realized that he couldn't risk being known as a Christian among the radical Muslims in Hamas. He was converted to Christ when he read the text, "Love your enemies." This belief was far more radical for him than that of the most radical Muslims. Our ministry helped him leave Palestine, and he now lives in the United States. His story has been told by major news organizations and can be found on YouTube under the title "Son of Hamas."

During another visit to Palestine, I was asked to meet with two Christian converts who had been part of Hamas. They told me of their struggles to live as Christians and as members of Hamas. They had told no one of their conversion. Shortly thereafter, I met with two more young Christian men from Hamas. They did not know—and did not want to know—whether there were any other Christians in Hamas. For the security of their fellow Christians, they refused to hear about any other believers whom they might compromise.

In Palestine it has happened that a Christian Jewish soldier is thrown into a situation in which he must search or even shoot an Arab Palestinian Christian. I know of one young Christian Jewish soldier who was searching for weapons in a Palestinian house. He noticed a cross and other signs of Christian faith in the home, but could not admit to being a fellow believer while serving as an Israeli soldier.

In 1947 nearly half the population of Jerusalem was Christian, but due to Israeli persecution Christians constitute only about 3 percent of Jerusalem's population today.[10] Many Arab and even Christian Jews are oppressed within the state of Israel. They face land confiscation, the arbitrary denial of building permits, confiscation of identity cards, and isolation behind walls that cut through their orchards and vineyards. Israelis use all means, both legal and illegal, to gain control of land. Jewish lawyers use Israeli law, British law, or even laws from the Ottoman period to suit their purpose of land confiscation. If these law codes do not support them, they are willing to build settlements illegally, while the Western world shakes its fists or wrings its hands.

As a result of this oppression, thousands of Palestinian Christians have migrated, leaving very few Christians in Palestine today. Afif Safieh, the former Palestinian ambassador to the United Kingdom and the Holy See, reported to the World Council of Churches that "you have many more Christian Palestinians in Chile than you have in Palestine; you have many more Christians *from* Jerusalem living in Sydney, Australia, than you have Christians *in* Jerusalem."[11]

Arabs can perhaps be excused for blaming anything that goes wrong on the Israelis. If someone stubs a toe, they blame an Israeli for putting the rock in their path. Many conspiracy theories have been spread about Israel. According to them, whatever evil happens in the Middle East can probably be traced back to the sinister workings of the Mossad and the CIA. Some are very creative in formulating stories about the evil plots that have been hatched by Jews, Americans, and "Crusaders." One of my recent favorites is the conspiracy theory about the Israelis and Americans starting the revolution in Egypt. To inspire the revolutionaries, the Americans allegedly bribed Kentucky Fried Chicken franchises in Egypt to give away free food to anyone who was willing to fight for independence.

Nonetheless, in Israel I also had one of the most moving spiritual experiences of my lifetime. I went to a Christian Jewish church that Muslim Arab converts also attended. One or two of the young Israelis present there had recently served in the Israeli army. I shared what Christ was doing among other Arab Muslims in front of the congregation. They asked to pray for me, gathered around me, and prayed in Arabic, Hebrew, and English. I wept. These historic enemies were united in Christ, and I now had Jewish brothers and sisters instead of Jewish enemies.

The Jewish Christians in that congregation also came to the aid of their Arab Christian brothers. They helped them financially and materially. They worshiped together and celebrated the Communion of the body of Christ together. I could not believe all the false hatred for these people that had been engendered in me from my childhood; it was as if a dam had broken. I saw that, in Christ, all truly can be one. I now believe that there can be peace in the Middle East only through Christ. Political solutions provide truces that are inevitably broken, but Christ provides mutual love and lasting reconciliation.

In spite of all these difficult issues of politics and identity, while I was in Israel, I saw the perfect model of what I believe needs to happen. I attended another mixed congregation of Messianic Jews and Arab Christians. The Jewish Christians washed the feet of their Arab brothers and sisters, and asked for forgiveness for the actions that the state of Israel had perpetrated against them. In turn, their Arab Christian brothers and sisters asked forgiveness for the centuries of hate they held for the Jews. Christ's forgiveness and love once again overcame.

CHAPTER TWELVE

MARRIAGE
and
FAMILY
in
ISLAM

I visited my sister in Egypt in 2005. We met well away from our childhood home in Cairo so no one would recognize me. As is customary, I had a gift for her: this time it was a modest French perfume. She graciously thanked me for it, noting that it was a kind of perfume that she couldn't get in Egypt. She then said, "I'll put it on at night—before I go to bed."

"What?" I asked in disbelief. "Why would you perfume yourself so that only you can smell it for a few minutes before you go to sleep? Why not put it on in the morning so that you can smell pleasant all day?"

"I might tempt a man if I did that," she responded.

I laughed out loud.

"You're almost sixty years old! You've never been named 'Miss Cairo.' Who would desire you? Do you really think that the men of Egypt are at a great risk of falling into sin if they get a whiff of your French perfume?"

She grabbed a wooden spoon from the kitchen and chased me around her house till we both burst into laughter.

But her attitude was that of a good Muslim woman, and it was typical. If a man is tempted, it's the woman's fault. Because of this, women are typically punished for adultery, while their male partners are not. And this is why women cover up with long gowns and veils in conservative Islamic nations. It is a woman's duty to protect a man from his own lust. When Arab men see Western television or travel to the West, they are stunned by what they view as the flagrant sexual openness of the women.

Westerners often view Arab women as abused girls who were forced to marry in their early teens and then wear a veil forever after—which is clearly a stereotype. Nonetheless, Arab women usually face more hardships than do Western women, and it is because of the inherent sexism of Islam. For example, in the year 2010, 47 percent of all marriages in Qatar were among blood relatives,[1] and it is quite unlikely that the young women had much choice in the matter. This percentage is probably about the same throughout much of the Arab world. Parents desire to guard the family and cultural customs, and marrying within the family is one of the best ways of keeping the family together. As I mentioned earlier, this was the case in my own family.

There are three steps in the Egyptian wedding process. First, there is the betrothal. The groom to be and the father of the bride shake hands with an elegant handkerchief between the hands. They recite the first chapter of the Qur'an and agree that the bride is now betrothed to the man. Four witnesses are required at this event. For my brother Moustafa and his bride to be, this period lasted six years. The second step is the "Writing of the Book": this is a written and legal statement that includes information about the dowry that the groom will pay, and even stipulates what will happen to the dowry and other goods in case of divorce. In this step the bride and groom say, "I give myself to you in marriage according to the tenets of Allah and his Messenger." Even here, the bride may have a male representative stand in for her. But this still does not mean the two are living together as husband and wife. This can be done if the families really want to be guaranteed of the marriage. It is after the third step, a celebratory feast, when the bride and groom consummate the marriage and move in together.

These three steps can occur on the same day, or they can be spread out over years. On the day of the wedding celebration, the bride will receive her dowry from the groom's parents. This becomes her personal property. The wedding contract is then a kind of prenuptial agreement that stipulates what will belong to the woman in case of divorce. Since there is, in principle, the possibility that the man may take more wives, there are no vows that promise exclusive commitment and love.[2]

My sister, Azieza, also married her cousin, another child of Uncle Sai'id. While doing his doctorate in France, Uncle Sai'id married a pretty Czech woman. She too was a Muslim, so there was no issue between them on that score, and Uncle Sai'id was said to have been deeply in love with her. She died in childbirth, but her baby son survived, and this was the older cousin my sister married. He was raised by a stepmother (Uncle Sai'id's second wife) who didn't treat him well, so he was happy to get out of that house and marry my sister. He too became a very successful civil engineer.

My brother Moustafa married outside the family. He was working in Algiers and met an Egyptian woman who was teaching there. They married, in spite of the fact that my mother already had a cousin from her side of the family picked out for him. The girl I fell in love with when I was about nineteen was my sister-in-law and first cousin, another daughter of Uncle Sai'id. Had I married her, we would have been three for four in marrying the children of Uncle Sai'id.

The view of women in Islam is much the same as it was in seventh-century Arabia. As was true of biblical times, that culture was very patriarchal. Inheritance passed through the line of the males, and sons were considered far more desirable than daughters. Christian theologians today widely affirm gender equality and extend it to home and workplace. Muslim theologians may note that the Qur'an says that men and women were created from "a single soul" (sura 4:1). Nonetheless, they argue that women should have little voice in the public square or mosque, and be submissive at home. Women are ceremonially unclean when they have their periods, so they cannot worship during those days.

Whereas many Christian feminists have gone on to distinguished careers in academic theology, female Islamic scholars are extraordinarily scarce, no doubt due to the cultural hold that patriarchy maintains in Arab lands. Muslim women face hardships at home, in the marketplace, and in their mosques that Christian women in the West do not.

Though it may sound unlikely, Muhammad was something of a reformer for women in his day. He forbade female infanticide, which was common in Arabia, and encouraged men to marry their servants or concubines rather than simply use them. Most of the wives he married after his first wife's death were widows, whose support he then undertook. Nonetheless, the view and treatment of women is what you would expect in the ancient Near East: women are of far lesser value than men and have far fewer rights and privileges. In one hadith, for example, Muhammad says that if a dog or a woman crosses a man's path when he is praying, the prayer is nullified.[3]

Much of the remaining negative view of women stems from the life and teachings of Muhammad himself, which is found in the hadiths, rather than the Qur'an. Orphaned at age six, Muhammad was raised by his paternal grandfather for two years and then, upon his grandfather's death, by his paternal uncle, Talib. Muhammad gained a reputation as an honest and wise young man, even earning the nickname "Trustworthy One." He traveled in his uncle's caravans that crossed the Arabian Desert into Syria, and his industriousness came to the attention of a wealthy widow named Khadija. Khadija hired Muhammad as her commercial agent and was so impressed with his integrity that she later proposed marriage to him. Though she was approximately fifteen years his senior, the happy marriage lasted until her death. Muhammad and Khadija had four daughters who survived infancy and two sons who did not.

When the young Muhammad began to have his divine visions, Khadija encouraged him, and even took him to see her Christian uncle to confirm their validity. After Khadija's death, Muhammad remarried a number of women in quick succession, eventually becoming a polygamist with a dozen or so wives. Muhammad, however, limited his followers to four wives at a time. And that is the practice that remains current in Islam today.

The last of Muhammad's wives was Aisha, the daughter of his friend and follower Abu Bakr. Aisha was nine years old when

Muhammad saw her playing on a swing, and she was betrothed to him. When she was twelve the marriage was consummated. There are stories of Muhammad happily carrying his very young wife on his shoulders. And she did make him happy. Other hadiths reported that the best time to see Muhammad was shortly after he had visited Aisha's tent. As a result of Muhammad's personal practice of marriage, conservative Islamists today still believe that girls can be married as young as age nine. And since Muhammad was fifty when this marriage was consummated, an enormous age gap between husband and wife is also seen as appropriate.

Women are not permitted to practice their faith in exactly the same way as men. They are not permitted to touch a Qur'an, enter the main section of the mosque for Friday prayers, offer liturgical prayers, or fast during Ramadan if they are having their period.[4] When my sister had her period during Ramadan, for example, she had to make up the time of fasting later. She could do it on her own schedule though, whether that was for a week straight, or for seven days scattered through seven months.

A small percentage of Arab women are highly educated and active in public, especially in the Gulf States. Some of these women refuse to marry. Why should they? If they marry this year, their husband may take a younger wife a few years later. They would also likely have to give up their careers as professionals.

A number of foreign women in the Gulf States live as virtual slaves while serving as domestic laborers. Most of them are not of Arab origin, though their families may have been in the Arabian Peninsula for generations. But between these two extremes, most women live in homes with their children, while their husbands try to earn enough income to maintain the family. Their neighbors, especially in smaller towns, are often relatives. Like women everywhere, most women in Arab lands struggle with the normal facets of family and social life.

For a brief moment during the Arab Spring, women came to the fore as fellow protesters. Women and men worked side by side in Tahrir Square to bring down the government. Shortly after the protests, however, the gender roles reasserted themselves. Rights for women have been placed on the back burner while the men fight for power. At present only eight out of 508 representatives in the Egyptian parliament are women.

Hopes for increased women's rights are often founded on increased education for women. This, again, has a mixed history in Egypt. When I was a student at the University of Cairo, about 40 percent of my fellow students were women. When the Muslim Brotherhood gained more control they quickly shut down the opportunities for women in education. This discrimination again peaked when the Brotherhood candidate Mohamed Morsi became prime minister in 2012. It pains me to see how much harm comes to Egyptian women when Islamists gain power.

In Islam a man may divorce his wife by openly and officially renouncing her three times, as was also true in ancient Israel. Infidelity is certainly one reason for divorce, but infertility, failure to produce a male child, or constant "disobedience" also qualify. Countries such as Egypt are now demanding that the couple go to court and attempt reconciliation rather than follow this old tradition. In fact, Egypt is one of the few Arab countries that permits women to legally divorce their husbands. In most of the Muslim world a woman is not allowed to divorce a man for any reason, with the possible exception of abandonment. If she does divorce him, she may very well forfeit all her rights and property. Should there be a divorce, the husband may claim the children when they reach the age of puberty, since they are legally his property. Alimony is provided according to the stipulations of the original marriage agreement and depends on the length of the marriage. I have sometimes wondered if the reason Arab men need so many social and legal advantages over women is that they are wimps. They may rightly fear that the women would take over if they had equal rights.

Both of my brothers experienced divorce. Yasser became so successful as a military dentist that he neglected his family and spent his time at the hospital, not at home. His wife asked him for a divorce; he reluctantly granted it to her, also permitting her to keep the children. He was devastated by the divorce from the woman he had grown up with, and by the loss of his two daughters. He moved back in with my mother for a time. I'm told he could often be found sobbing on her shoulder. Obviously, this break in the marriage also created a new rift in the extended family as well, since he was divorcing his cousin.

My brother Moustafa was divorced twice. He had two girls and one boy with his first wife, and things seemed to go well for many years. He was a wonderful father to his three children, but his Egyptian wife was quite domineering. It may be that my conversion contributed to the rift between them: she thought I was a traitor or a spy, and Moustafa often came to my defense. After decades of marriage, she too asked for a divorce. Moustafa rationalized that since she had been a good mother to their children, he ought to let her go without a fight. After they divorced he quickly remarried the wrong woman. He divorced her shortly after, and has been single ever since.

My sister, Azieza, never divorced, but she did live apart from her husband for a lengthy period. On one of my visits to Egypt, I spoke with her and her estranged husband about this. I asked why they continued to live apart from each other after so many years. Wouldn't it make more sense to pay for only one house and to be together for the children? After I spoke to both of them, they did move back in together. He however has recently died.

It is generally assumed that Muslim women will get married and have children. That is the primary role they are expected to fulfill. In Islam the husband is the legal owner of his wife's body,[5] and therefore he may demand sexual access to her at any time he wishes—except in times of ritual impurity. The husband is expected to provide materially for the family, though today many Muslim women work outside of their homes. The world of women is separated from that of men. Women are typically in the home; when they do go out, it is to buy food, clothing, and other necessities for the home. In some countries, such as Saudi Arabia, the women don't even go out alone when they go to the market. In other places, such as upscale Cairo, they can be seen out on the streets at night.

Islam has a difficult time understanding and responding to the Western view of love and romance that is seen in so much of the media. One example is Valentine's Day. The day is named for a Christian saint, Valentine, and celebrates the love that men and women have for each other. But since it is a Christian holiday, and celebrates emotional and physical love, most imams want nothing to do with it. In fact, one imam in Saudi Arabia delivered a Valentine fatwa that forbade any celebration of Valentine's Day. Some Saudis objected, saying it was only right that spouses express their love for one another. But the imam held firm, instructing the police to stop any and all Valentine's Day practices. As a result, on Valentine's Day in Saudi Arabia you can find men clandestinely buying chocolates, flowers, and cards for their wives, all the while looking over their shoulders for the police.

Even so, romance and marriage are a common theme in the Arab media. An Egyptian soap opera titled *The Family of Hajji Mitwali* uses polygamy as the point of tension in its plot. Hajji Mitwali has four wives.[6] How will they get along? Will they become friends, all sharing in various household duties and sexual favors? Or will they become rivals? Four women in one house certainly provide ample opportunity for plot twists and turns, and the series has gone on for years. In theory, a Muslim man could even have more than four wives if he divorced one wife before taking on wife five, and so on.[7] (Polyandry, however, is not permitted.)

Many Arabs who watch TV shows such as these believe it is better for a man to have four wives than to have one wife who he constantly cheats on, which is what they see on Western television. They also point out that in times of war, when many men die, it is better that the remaining men should take on another wife than let the widows succumb to prostitution.

Given the fact that polygamy was practiced at some times in the biblical narrative, I grant that there may be instances when polygamy may be the lesser of evils. But this is not how polygamy usually works in Arab lands. There, typically only the few men who can financially afford a second, third, or fourth wife will take them to serve their self-esteem and libido. My nephew, my sister's son, has had multiple wives and divorces. The conflict from all of this has caused Azieza daily grief.

Countries—and even ethnic groups within countries—vary in their treatment of women. For example, rules about women's coverings vary widely. In countries like Saudi Arabia or Afghanistan, the veil (*niqab*) covers everything but the eyes. In others, such as Turkey, a head scarf is enough. In some countries, even a woman's voice is thought to be too provocative to be heard in public; in others, women's voices are heard throughout the marketplace. The Qur'an insists that women dress modestly, and in 1 Corinthians 11:5 St. Paul too recommends that women cover their heads. But whereas modern Christians recognize this as an appropriate cultural practice for the first century CE, they do not see it as a universal rule. Since the Qur'an, however, is understood as one single, infallible whole, it is difficult for its scholars to sort out its ancient cultural customs from its lasting truths. Today, in Egypt, due to the influence of the Muslim Brotherhood and other conservative Islamic groups, women must cover more of their bodies than they did thirty years ago.

A woman's covering can lead to some interesting cultural quirks. When I was in college I knew a brother and sister who were both accounting students. The brother had graduated, and the sister needed to take an exam he had already passed. The brother donned a woman's veil and covering and took the exam for her. The teacher suspected something when she saw a large hairy hand writing the exam, so she took the "woman" aside and asked her to take off the veil. He was caught.

Unfortunately, women continue to endure the practice of circumcision, or female genital mutilation, in some Islamic nations. Though it is not mandated in the Qur'an, it is still practiced in many African and Arab countries. (Asian Muslims are not so apt to perform circumcision on their daughters.) The idea behind female circumcision is that a man's lust must be held in check by removing the sexual desire of women. A woman must not tempt men. Cutting the clitoris is seen as a way of ensuring this. Obviously, this is a perverse view of women's sexuality and a horrifying experience for young women to endure. What's more, it is done for the benefit of the men, with the sole goal of protecting their souls from temptation.

CHAPTER THIRTEEN

CHRISTIAN–
MUSLIM FAMILIES

According to the Qur'an and the hadiths, a Muslim man may take a Christian or Jewish wife. These women are considered "People of the Book" and thus closer to Islam than polytheistic pagans. In fact, this tradition goes back to Muhammad himself, who had both a Christian and a Jewish wife. When a Muslim man does marry a woman of the Book, their children are automatically Muslim through him. The reverse, however, does not hold true. A Christian man may not take a Muslim woman as wife and make her and the children Christian; it is simply not legally permitted. The law in Egypt recognizes only marriages between two Muslims or between two Coptic Christians as legitimate; children of the former are Muslims and those of the latter are Christians.[1]

When Muslim women convert to Christianity they face great hardships. They could lose their children, their alimony, and their inheritance—in other words, everything. Yet many do come to Christ. Those who do are invariably strong in faith, and their commitment to Christ is firm. Many of the male converts, on the other hand, are wishy-washy. They may become Christians, but then renounce their faith when they see the price they must pay.

In my own family, the people who know I am a Christian don't tell their friends or children. If they did, they would risk losing potential marriage partners. My sister-in-law, for example, has never told her daughters about me. The whispers would begin, "Her uncle is an apostate." It would bring them shame to acknowledge this part of the family background. Decades after my conversion I was able to visit my mother's family village along with my wife and daughter. I made sure they dressed very modestly. They wore knee-length skirts and tops with high necklines. My daughter Becky got along very well with her cousins, so they dressed her up in an Egyptian peasant woman's dress. It covered her from head to toe. I am happy to report that she is still in touch with those cousins via Facebook.

Thanks to the fact that I was legally adopted by an American couple, I can now travel safely back to Egypt—as well as to other countries in the Middle East—on an American passport. It is odd, and indeed providential, to see how that worked out. Whereas the adoption didn't serve its original purpose of getting me a US visa when I was in my twenties, it does help me get visas in the Middle East some thirty years later. I go through the immigration lines in Egypt and they ask me, "Were you born in Egypt?" "Yes," I reply. "Is your father Egyptian?"[2] "No," I answer in honesty and in legal fact. "Okay. Welcome to Egypt."

On one trip to Egypt, I met a nephew I hadn't seen for years. He is about ten years younger than I and had looked up to me when he was a child. He told me that after I fled Egypt, the kids in the neighborhood would jeer and spit at him when he walked down the street. "Your uncle is an apostate! He's a stinking dog!" I felt bad. There was no way my sweet nephew should have had to pay for my decision. I was saddened but not entirely surprised to learn that my conversion had caused him this abuse. Another nephew I had talked to about Christ reacted by turning deeper into Islam. He sometimes now acts as a Muslim street preacher.

I also learned that my entire family came under suspicion by the secret police. My mother's mail was opened before she got it, and family members were spied on. The secret police wanted to be certain that a subversive Christian movement wasn't sprouting up in our home. Muslim society often views the Christians within it as a cancerous tumor that should be cut out as quickly as possible. If my family had become Christian, they too would have been killed or persecuted. I didn't think of it at the time, but my leaving Islam put my family at risk. It also disgraced them. Thirty years later my mother was still referred to as "the mother of the apostate." Mine was not the only family to face this problem; converts from Islam are always considered a shame to their families. If individuals become Christians, they are ostracized or even killed by their family. If the entire family becomes Christian, the broader society ostracizes or kills them. For this reason many Muslim converts keep their Christian faith a secret.

Another of my nephews is blond, no doubt thanks to his European grandmother, and being a blond in Egypt is considered quite a distinction. A young woman in his neighborhood was pregnant and hoped to have a blond child of her own. She found my nephew and put some honey in his hand. She then licked the honey out of his hand, believing that this would reproduce my nephew's blond hair in her baby. There are a lot of popular folk practices like this that persist in Arab lands, and trying to understand them in a rational, Western way just doesn't work. That is also why arguing with Muslims about Christ is rarely a successful strategy. "Who cares if you can make a good Western argument?" What normally attracts Muslims to the Christian faith is the love of Christ as seen in his people. Rational explanations and justifications may come later, but an argument rarely brings about a conversion.

Converts to Christianity in Egypt must remain Muslims in every legal sense because their fathers were Muslims. So neither men nor women converts are permitted to officially change their religion. During an Egyptian marriage ceremony each partner must say the shahada, "There is one God, Allah, and Muhammad is his Prophet," as well as recite the first chapter of the Qur'an. So even if both the woman and the man are now Christians, the marriage ceremony is Islamic, and the couple remains Muslim according to the law. What can Christian couples do? I have seen pairs of Muslim converts to Christianity get married in a third country, someplace where Christian marriages are permitted. They then register their Christian marriage in their home country and move back there. Obviously, not every pair of Muslim converts who wish to marry can do this.

It is difficult for Muslim converts to find appropriate marriage partners, since so many of them keep their faith secret. Women find this situation especially hard. Their parents push them to get married, and sometimes even try to arrange a marriage for them with a Muslim man. Even if the Muslim husband permits her to go to church or have women friends who are Christian, the children will necessarily be Muslim. When a daughter from such a marriage comes of age, the potential husband will likely insist that she wear the hijab or face female circumcision. When a boy comes of age he will be taken to the mosque each Friday and expected to perform the pillars of Islam. Christian women who marry Muslim men lead extremely difficult lives.

It can even be difficult for a male convert to Christianity to marry a woman who is Christian if his family remains Muslim. Imagine sitting around the dinner table at his parents' house on Friday afternoon after mosque. The Christian grandson asks Grandpa if he can pray before the meal. Muslim grandpa is pleased until he hears the prayer: "God bless this food and drink, in Jesus' name. Amen." This has actually occurred, and there was an uproar over the words "in Jesus' name." On Sunday the same family may visit the mother's family after church. There, a prayer in Jesus' name will win the approval of all. On Monday in school, other kids might beat him up, as I did to the Christian kids when I was a schoolboy. What will such a child do? One such child began to wet his bed again at age eight due to the stress and the fear. To spare their child such persecution, another couple I know decided to raise their children as cultural Muslims, hoping that they would make a decision for Christ when they came of age.

There is really no such thing as adoption in Islam, and the absence of it goes back to Muhammad himself. Muhammad once adopted a young man named Yazeed. Yazeed married a beautiful young woman. One day when Muhammad went to Yazeed's tent to visit his son, the tent flap blew open, and Muhammad saw his daughter-in-law undressed. He desired her as his wife and compelled Yazeed to divorce her in order that he could marry her. But to make it look right, Muhammad claimed that he had never really adopted Yazeed, though in fact earlier he had said Yazeed was "*like* a son to me." Muhammad later received another Quranic revelation that said the adopted son was not a true son for Muhammad (sura 33:37-41), providing a useful after-the-fact sanction for his actions. To this day then, Muslims will not adopt each other's children. If a child's parents die, the next closest relatives take the child in. If none of them can afford to do so, the child may become a street child.

Christian organizations sometimes build orphanages to care for these street children in Arab lands. They often try to have the children adopted either nationally or internationally. In more than one country, however, the government believes that the orphanages are a cover for Christian evangelism and closes them.

Muhammad said that women are "lacking in common sense and failing in religion."[3] As a result, women are not granted full rights in Islam, and the testimony of two women is required to equal that of one man. One Egyptian columnist noted that the testimony of one woman who is a doctor is worth half that of a man who peddles oranges. It's true. Even in death women are treated unequally. Women enter paradise, but their lot is hardly the equivalent of men. Muhammad said, "I was shown the hell of fire, and that the majority of its dwellers are women."[4] When a man gets to paradise, he will receive seventy virgins with "plump breasts" to serve him, plus the wives he had on this earth. When a woman makes it to heaven, she goes as the wife and servant of the man. These conditions caused my sister to admit, "We Muslim women lose out in both this life and the next. We're damned both on earth and in heaven."

If a woman who is a Christian convert from Islam marries a Coptic man, their marriage is not considered legal. They are technically "living in sin" according to Islamic law, and the marriage could be annulled by other family members. They could even have their children taken away from them. The only legal Christian marriage in Egypt must be between two people who were born Copts. The Copts, however, do not permit divorce among their members, so when a Coptic couple needs to get a divorce, they typically leave the church first. After they have become a Protestant, or perhaps even a Muslim, they go ahead with the divorce.

The very worst marriage-related case I know of involved a Muslim woman convert to Christianity; she had achieved a great deal as a surgeon. Her family remained Muslim. They knew that if a non-Muslim woman is raped by a Muslim man, the baby that may result will necessarily be Muslim and be considered as property of the man.[5] So when this doctor's family discovered that she had become a Christian, both her father and her brother raped her—to guarantee that she would not have a Christian child. The fact that she had been raped also made it socially impossible for her to marry another man, ruined her career, and destroyed her emotionally.

In fairness, I should also mention the best case I have heard. There was a Christian woman of Muslim background whose well-to-do family disapproved of her decision to accept Christ. They compelled her to marry a Muslim man, who beat her and made her life hell—so she divorced him. She later remarried, this time to a Christian man. By that time, her family was not only supportive and enthusiastic, but provided them with gifts and welcomed him into their family.

The pressure on women to get married is greater than that placed on men—in Egypt and no doubt elsewhere. Women have the biological clock that ticks off the years of childbearing, and like women everywhere, Egyptian women love their children and grand-children. Men see less urgency in getting married, and Arab Christian men know that marriage to a Christian woman may entail a host of social and family problems. Thus the number of eligible Christian women in Arab lands is relatively higher than that of men.

To help some of these dear women, I have done a bit of match-making. It's not as if I sit in a village like the old woman in *Fiddler on the Roof*, waiting for people to bring me gifts for a dowry—but I do make connections. I sometimes know of believing men who are not so distant from the women, but who may not have gone public with their faith. Or sometimes I know of a single Christian man from their ethnic group who lives in another country and would like to get married. I introduce them in person or online. I have conducted a number of weddings for these couples. In fact, I may have performed the first-ever wedding in which the bride and groom, as well as the pastor, were all Muslim converts. Marriage in any circumstance is not easy, and marriage as a religious minority in a hostile land is especially difficult. But by God's grace, Christian marriages and families in Arab lands can survive and even thrive, to the glory of God.

CHAPTER FOURTEEN

EGYPT NOW

Living in Egypt from 2011 to the present has been like riding a rollercoaster. Three presidents, two revolutions, a couple of constitutions, and numerous demonstrations have made life more interesting than most would wish.

My brother was in Tahrir Square when the first revolution against Mubarak occurred. I myself was in Egypt a couple of weeks later and talked with Moustafa. He gave me a detailed chronology of where the battles were being fought, who was involved, who had been killed, and what he had done. He said that the revolution was largely brought about by social media. The original protesters were young people who organized via Facebook and other media sources. They determined online when they would meet and what they would do, and then created the protests and other events. This continued to the very evening of Mubarak's overthrow. My brother was on his cell phone all night, in contact with other protesters. They would text each other about which streets had police on them, which were barricaded, and which were controlled by the protesters. One Egyptian family was so grateful for the role Facebook played in the revolution that they named their new daughter Facebook.

I was envious that Moustafa got to be at the center of the action for this historical event. Though he was in his sixties at the time, he told me he had never run so fast in his life than when he was fleeing the army in Tahrir Square that night. It was amazing to see the smiles on the faces of the average people, and the pride they had in their young revolutionaries. Egypt had revolutions and coups before, but they were usually led by the military. This one was led by the people themselves. Though I was living in the United States at the time, I bought an Egyptian flag and yelled "Viva Egypt!" All around the world, Egyptians like myself were glued to the TV to see what was going on. During the demonstrations, television and online viewers could see one of the offices of the secret police burning. It was not the protestors who burned it, however. The secret police themselves burned it down to make sure that the records of what they had done would not survive.

To explain why the revolution occurred requires going back in time to the first person named in this story—Gamal Abdel Nasser. When he and the other Free Officers overthrew King Farouk in 1952, they changed Egypt forever. Like most other nations emerging from colonial power, Egypt would never be a monarchy again. But what would it be: a democracy, a dictatorship, an oligarchy, a military state, or an Islamic theocracy?

Twenty-eight years earlier, an Egyptian schoolteacher by the name of Hassan al-Banna started the Muslim Brotherhood. It began as an Islamic renewal movement in Egypt. But by the time Nasser became president it had become a secretive organization with cells and centers throughout the Arabic-speaking world. When King Farouk was overthrown, the Muslim Brotherhood had a very clear idea of what they wanted Egypt to become—an Islamist state. They felt that to uphold true Islam they needed to install sharia law and a caliph who would rule the Arab world as a Muslim leader.

Nasser was certainly a Muslim. But he was not the kind of Muslim who wanted to institute sharia law for all of society or lock women up in their homes or behind veils. He was a progressive who worked for Arab unity and against Western imperialism. He walked the line between capitalism and communism, but leaned strongly toward the socialism of the Soviet Union. He was a charismatic leader. I still have recordings of his speeches that I turn to for inspiration. His Arabic prose is equal to the English speeches of Winston Churchill or Martin Luther King Jr.

The Brotherhood soon realized that their hopes for an Islamic state in Egypt would never come to fruition under Nasser, so they plotted his assassination. Nasser himself got wind of this. As a military man, he was quite decisive. He immediately killed off many of the conspirators, including Hassan al-Bana himself, and sent thousands of the Muslim Brothers to prison. I had a cousin who got caught up in this. His name apparently was on the ledgers of the Muslim Brotherhood as having given twenty-five piasters (maybe about fifty cents at that time) to the Brotherhood as a charitable donation. Nasser's men got hold of the Brotherhood's records that included his name. He disappeared for years. We didn't know exactly what happened to him, but we knew it was not good.

Given its oppression by the Nasser regime, the Brotherhood had to become an underground organization. They could not meet or organize openly. But they were always around. Admittedly, they did some good. They helped the poor by building schools, factories, and hospitals. They became active in the businesses and professions of Egypt. They bowed to the ground in prayer so often that their foreheads had little bumps on them that we called raisins. They were especially eager to control the educational system. They believed, correctly it turns out, that they could inculcate their ideology in the young so that later they would have a pool of recruits for their Islamist revolution. To accomplish this they instituted *madrasas* (Islamic schools) that taught young boys Islamist doctrine.

Nasser died of natural causes in 1970, and his vice president, Anwar Sadat, became president. Sadat did not have the support of Nasser's socialist backers, who tried to oust him from the presidency. Before they could, Sadat released the members of the Muslim Brotherhood so they would be free to help him against the socialists. The Brotherhood was then out in the open again and became a vital force in Egypt during the 1970s when Sadat was in power. Sadat installed a version of sharia law, purged the secret police Nasser had set up, and cut ties with the Soviet Union. He gave the Copts and other Egyptian Christians a hard time. It seemed that he was doing everything the Brotherhood wanted. He then signed a famous peace treaty with Israel at Camp David. This, however, was not at all what the Islamists had in mind. One of them from a radical group called the Egyptian Islamic Jihad assassinated Sadat in 1981.

Finally, we arrive at Hosni Mubarak, who ruled from 1982 till 2011. Mubarak was also a military man and was Sadat's vice president. He was with Sadat when Sadat was assassinated, and was wounded in the hand during the gunfire. It soon became apparent that he was not going to allow himself to be assassinated by fringe Islamists. He purged the government of anyone suspected of being a radical Islamist, banned the Brotherhood from public life, and vastly increased the power of the internal security forces. He jailed anyone who was believed to be involved in the conspiracy, including Ayman al-Zawahri. The name Zawahri may be familiar to you as the head of al-Qaeda after the death of Osama bin Laden. Zawahri became involved in al-Qaeda after serving four miserable and tortured years in Egyptian prisons under Mubarak. He and others like him were radicalized while in prison. He came to believe that there could be no compromise with secular or Western nations. Only a true Islamic state was acceptable, and terrorism against the infidels was the only way to bring it about. Ayman al-Zawahri was known to our family since he was my brother's classmate in high school.

Mubarak was a military man whose rule grew constantly more dictatorial. When he entered office, half of the Egyptian population lived in poverty, and when he left, they still did, while Mubarak's family and friends lived lavishly. So the revolution against him was a genuine people's rebellion against oppression. It arose when Egyptians came to understand that they could take charge of their own destiny as had protesters in Tunisia, Syria, and Yemen. Mubarak was ousted by popular revolt in 2011. Since the Muslim Brotherhood had been an established political entity for decades, they quickly emerged as the most effective, organized group among the protesters. But socialists like my brother, Coptic Christians, and others who were sick of the corruption and oppression under Mubarak were also a large part of that uprising.

In fact, this was the first time Christians were visibly present during an uprising in Egypt. A common phrase in Arabic is "Walk close to the wall," which is the rough equivalent of "Keep your head down." In Egypt, Christians have "walked close to the wall" for centuries, but this time they were open in their support of the revolution. During the revolution, Muslims continued to observe their times of prayer. But while they were kneeling toward Mecca to pray, they would be vulnerable to attacks from the police. So some Christians formed a circle around the Muslims when the Muslims held their daily prayers. Christian churches served as clinics for the wounded, never asking what the wounded believed. Christian churches also held memorial services for the Muslims who were killed by the government. For many at these services, this was the first and only time they had ever been in a church. One Christian pastor preached a sermon titled "Oh Egypt, I Love You," and Muslims and Christians together sang hymns. It was the first time the Christian church was so clearly a welcomed part of Egyptian life since 1919, when a Coptic priest and a Muslim imam walked arm in arm to protest the injustices of the king.[1]

Previously, Egyptian Muslims thought that Christians could not truly be patriotic Egyptians, since they had other allegiances. After the Iraq war, some Egyptians even feared that the presence of Christians in Egypt would serve as a pretext for the United States to get involved militarily during the Egyptian revolution. But the Christians in Cairo dispelled all these myths. They were as loyal to our country as any.

After the revolution, the Brotherhood, through its political wing called the Freedom and Justice Party, won a fair election. Muhammad Morsi, a card-carrying Muslim Brotherhood member, was elected president of Egypt. This was what the Brotherhood had been longing for since their formation in 1928. They won. They had a mandate to rule after an election that was internationally recognized as legitimate. Euphoria!

It didn't last a week. Immediately the Brotherhood took up the task of setting up a utopian Islamic state. Conceptually, this meant giving ultimate allegiance not to the nation of Egypt but to a metaphysical entity called the "Islamic World" or the "Islamic Umma" (People). This entity goes well beyond national boundaries and is conceptual rather than physical. So those who define what that concept is get to establish and regulate it. This meant a number of things, all of which were bad, at least from the perspective of Christians, Western democracies, and women. One reporter describes their tactics as follows:

> The Morsi administration and the Brotherhood governed in a unilateral fashion, employing a winner-take-all majoritarian view of their electoral gains that alienated parties from across the political spectrum—including erstwhile allies in the ultraconservative Salafi Nour Party—and prevented them from building trust among Egyptians outside of their traditional constituency. They opted not to engage in any meaningful consultations on state policy between the government and NGOs, civil society, activists and other stakeholders.[2]

First, they tried to eliminate or control cultural institutions not seen as fitting in an Islamic World. They replaced the "liberal" Minister of Culture with a man who was more to their liking. He showed his true spirit by quickly closing down the Egyptian Opera. He then went after a comedian, Adel Imam, who had written the comedic film *The Terrorist*, which was a spoof on radical Islam. I give the Brotherhood credit for knowing who and what shape culture; they got the right targets.

Then, women were of course subjugated. Female representation in parliament went from 12 percent to 2 percent, and the mandate requiring that sixty-five members of parliament be women was discarded. The Freedom and Justice party openly declared that a woman would never be president. They insisted that only civil laws that were in accord with sharia law would be considered valid. This gave them power to change laws regarding divorce, property ownership for women, and protection from spousal abuse. Again, give the Brotherhood credit; they realized that educated and forceful women were a threat to their power.

They then directed their vision of a pure Islamic state toward the tourism industry. The Brotherhood busied themselves with questioning whether Westerners could wear swimsuits along Egypt's Mediterranean beaches or shorts around the pyramids. They concluded that tourists should not, as it is against Islamic law. Tourism crashed. In 2008, before the revolutions, about twelve million tourists visited Egypt, and about 12 percent of the Egyptian workforce served tourism. After the first revolution and the Morsi election, tourism dropped by about a third, as did related employment.

To enforce the strict tourism rules, President Morsi appointed a new governor, Adel al-Khayat, in Luxor, the home of the pyramids and the sphinx. Khayat was a member of Gamaa Islamiya, the same radical Islamic group that claimed responsibility for the massacre of fifty-eight tourists in Luxor in 1997. Khayat himself was likely a participant in that massacre. So, instead of guaranteeing the safety of wealthy tourists who paid for 12 percent of Egypt's employment, Morsi appointed a man who was likely their assassin. This was too much for every sensible Egyptian. A coalition of opposition groups, trade unions, and tourism workers threatened to close down all pharaonic temples and tourist attractions if Khayat remained in his post. He was forced to resign within a week.

The economy was in a steady downward spiral, with inflation and unemployment on the rise. The Morsi government offered no clear plan for recovery other than a reliance on sporadic injections of cash from regional allies, Qatar chief among them.

An independent journalist describes the first year of President Morsi's rule:

Egypt's political fabric first began to come apart at the seams following Morsi's November 2012 constitutional declaration that granted him far-reaching powers and placed his decisions above judicial reach. This sparked the first mass protests against his rule, leading to clashes between his opponents and supporters. The Brotherhood then rammed through a constitution drafted by an assembly that had seen a walkout of all of its non-Islamist members, a move that polarized the political arena beyond repair. The Brotherhood's reluctance to engage in any kind of inclusive or consensual process left it politically isolated when dissenters began to coalesce against it.[3]

Not surprisingly, Christians were even more visible in the second revolution. They knew they were fighting for their lives. While Morsi ruled, St. Mark's Cathedral, the glorious and symbolic center of the Coptic Church, was the target of sectarian violence. Members who entered the cathedral to mourn those slain in the revolution were pelted with stones. Eighty-two Christian churches were burned down, and police fired tear gas at the members. The Brotherhood accused Christians of hiding weapons in the churches as an excuse for the burnings. Coptic women were urged to wear the Islamic veil. One fatwa even made it illegal for a Muslim to wish Christians "Merry Christmas." Some Christian business-people had to fold up shop since they were attacked with impunity. Christians were hardly the only ones who despised Morsi and the Brotherhood. The majority of Egypt was contemptuous.

Radical Islam showed its true colors after the first Egyptian revolution. The Morsi government was rightly ridiculed as incompetent. And woe to those who dared raise criticisms! In the first two hundred days of Morsi's presidency there were more lawsuits for "insulting the president" than there were during the entire thirty-year rule of Mubarak.[4] The protests against him were eventually greater in scale than those mounted against Mubarak. At one point there were as many as thirty-two million Egyptians protesting against Morsi, whereas the record number of protestors against Mubarak was two million. In one year's time President Morsi managed to alienate virtually all Egyptians who were not members of the Brotherhood. Exactly one year and three days after assuming office, Morsi was thrown out.[5]

Westerners wondered why we Egyptians were so fickle. We elected a man one year and deposed him the next. But Westerners, especially those in the United States, seem to think that having a free election equals having a democracy. It doesn't. Adolf Hitler won a free election too, and millions still rue the fact that the Germans did not depose him. The United States encouraged a free election in Palestine, and the most radical Islamist party— Hamas—won the election and made life miserable for Israel, the Western powers, and the Palestinians themselves. It doesn't matter that a person gets in to an office properly as much as it does that the person upholds that office properly. Morsi did not. He attempted to overthrow his own government and establish an Islamic dictatorship.

Beside the Brotherhood, the only other well-organized and politically powerful entity in Egypt is the military. So, along with the vast majority of Egyptians, the second revolution involved the military. During the Morsi administration the police and military were put in the awkward position of having to enforce policies they did not support. That sometimes entailed using force against protesters who were seeking the same things the police themselves wanted. The police were then held liable for the actions they were compelled to take. So when the public demanded that Morsi step down, General Abdel Fattah el-Sisi acceded to their calls and forced Morsi out. Elections in May 2014 then gave Sisi the presidency.

So we are in a similar situation to the one we were under Nasser; the military rules, and the Brotherhood is on the run or underground. The Brotherhood is out of power, out of favor, and an embarrassment. The Egyptian judiciary sided with Sisi and condemned to death five hundred members of the Brotherhood. I doubt they will actually be executed, but it sure does make a point. Egyptians, as well as most other Arab Muslims, now see just how bad an Islamic state can be. They see it in Egypt, they saw it in Iran, and they see it in ISIS (the Islamic State of Iraq and Syria). In all of these cases it is obvious that Muslims can be vicious toward one another while attempting to install the ideal Islamic state. An oft-quoted verse in the Qur'an tells Muslims, "You are the best nation produced [as an example] for mankind. You enjoin what is right and forbid what is wrong and believe in Allah. If only the People of the Scripture had believed, it would have been better for them. Among them are believers, but most of them are defiantly disobedient" (sura 3:110).

The "People of the Scripture" were the Christians. But now, many Muslims wonder whether the best nation is Christianity. One woman has said that the Qur'an got it wrong. The text, she thinks should read, "You (House of Islam) are the most evil nation ever produced as an example for mankind."[6]

Seeing full-blown Islam is a frightening and embarrassing experience. As I have said earlier, I believe that the radical Islamists are the real Muslims, and that the kind of theocratic state they seek to establish is the necessary outcome of orthodox Islam. Enforcing the dictates of the Qur'an as well as sharia law will happen automatically wherever Islam takes full control. The same rather bitter Muslim woman commented on her own faith in this way:

Isn't it shameful that after fourteen hundred years of Islamic traditions we Muslims still need a cane in order to walk? Because of the shameful behavior and opinions of our religious leaders we have become a laughingstock of the world, as if we were the theater's latest comedy. Some religious clerics have even managed to convert us into atheists! . . . How can there be Allah when killing and beheading and cutting toes and fingers and burning human beings is part of our Islamic belief? These things prove to the world that God is nowhere, and he does not care about what Muslims do. Look at Islam in Iraq—a continuous slaughter; Islam in Sudan has divided into North and South; Islam in Palestine is divided into Fatah and Hamas, and in my country [Egypt] into infidel Sunnis and infidel Shiites. Quit, oh Muslims, from defending Allah by killing people; rather, defend the souls of humanity so they can all get to know Allah. Will the prophet of Islam be happy and proud and excited by the many heads which have been cut off by Muslims when he sees this, or will he commit suicide from what he sees?[7]

Some argue that quotes like this one only refer to "radical" Islam, and that this is not necessarily what an Islamic state must be like. I disagree. Full-blown Islam will require sharia law, and it will derive its social customs from seventh-century Arabia. None of these are compatible with modern democracy. So Islam cannot reform itself in a way that will fit modern times. The Muslim countries that have gotten closest to an "ideal" Islamic state are the world's worst in terms of oppression and poverty. (Think of Saudi Arabia for oppression and Afghanistan for poverty.) Unfortunately, I don't see any changes in Islam that will make this situation better. In the past, those who have tried to reform Islam have been shut down or even killed. *Sunni* means the "trodden path," and that path is indeed well-worn. Adapting to modernity would require that Islam diverge from that path at right angles, something it is both unwilling and unable to do.[8] Islam has shut down nearly all efforts at sociopolitical change and shows no indications of changing directions. It's all or nothing, a true Islamic society with the caliphate or a secular and apostate one.

Many Muslims are saddened and bewildered, hurt and embarrassed by their brutal and ineffective leaders, and I feel sad and hurt with them. But I have a response I would like to share with them: the Prince of Peace, who gave his life for his friends, is available to them.

CHAPTER FIFTEEN

MUSLIM CONVERTS

More Muslims have come to Christ in the past forty years than did in the preceding fourteen hundred. We know this is true, though exact statistics are extremely difficult to find. For instance, among the Berber peoples in Algeria, tens of thousands have come to Christ. Twenty years ago there were next to none. The first Christian missionary work among the Berbers began in 1881, but few were converted. After Algeria's war of independence from France (1954–1962), many Berbers fled, and the French were expelled. One missionary who was forced to leave told an Algerian Christian woman, "This will be a black day in the history of Algeria." The woman, later known as the mother of the church of Algeria, prayed that it would not be. Her prayers were answered, and in the years following the expulsion of the Western missionaries, the church grew dramatically.

One likely reason the Berbers were so amenable to Christianity is their minority status in Islam. Arabic is not their first language, and Muslims believe that prayers and readings must be recited in Arabic. The Qur'an itself cannot be officially translated into other languages since only classical Arabic is considered to be its true language. When the Qur'an is unofficially translated into another language, it is typically labeled an "interpretation" and is given the lower status of the receptor language. The Qur'an has never even been "interpreted" into the main Berber tongues. But the Bible has been. In fact, the Bible was the first book to be written in a principal Berber tongue, and the first film in this Berber tongue was the *Jesus* film.[1]

The Berbers are ethnically distinct from the Arabs and are proud of their unique heritage. Non-Arabic Muslims throughout the world are often made to feel like second-class citizens in the House of Islam. So when the Bible became available to them, and they learned that they could be accepted for who they are as Berbers, they began to come to Christ in significant numbers. Many of these Berbers ended up in France, where they, in turn, became missionaries. Some Berber pastors now lead evangelical French congregations. The Berbers may be a great missional success story, but there are other lesser ones as well. I think there are three likely reasons.

First, it must simply be God's time. Since the death of the Prophet in 632 CE, Islam has spread and grown—and it continues to do so. Yet the number of Muslims who are coming to Christ is also growing. For hundreds of years the number of Christians in countries like Saudi Arabia was believed to be zero. But today we know that there are house churches in Mecca and Medina, the very centers of Islam. Perhaps in the same way that God prepared the world for the coming of the Messiah during the time of the Roman Empire, God has now prepared this time for Christ to come to the Muslims.

Second, prayer. I have it on good authority that as many as fifty million Christians throughout the world regularly pray for the Muslim world, and this number continues to increase.[2]

Finally, technology. Modern technologies can spread the gospel unimpeded. There are now Christian websites in Arabic that present the gospel daily. Programs on cable TV show Christian believers of Muslim background talking about their faith and their families. Radio broadcasts proclaim the faith in nearly all the Islamic dominant languages. In the past, Muslims believed there was no such thing as a Muslim convert to Christianity; it was unthinkable that anyone would leave the perfection of Islam for its misguided predecessor. Today, Muslim converts are on television and radio every day proclaiming their faith. Maintaining the pretension that no one has left Islam for Christianity has become difficult for even the most convicted Muslim.

Today copies of the Bible in Arabic and other Muslim dominant languages are available online, in print, and on flash drives. In most languages, including Arabic, biblical commentaries, Christian movies, music, and books are also available. We know that people are looking at these materials because the owners of the websites that provide them track thousands of hits.[3] It is, however, extremely difficult to know exactly how many people have actually become Christians as a result, since most new believers hide their newfound faith.

The beautiful role of music in Muslim evangelism should be noted. In Islam, music is not used in worship; in fact, the use of instruments and singing is banned within some Islamic groups.[4] This is why Muslims don't have a tradition of classical music or the equivalent of Handel's *Messiah* in Arabic. When Muslims come into contact with some of the inspirational and beautiful music of the church, they are awed. When they see that men and women can gather together and sing praises to God, they detect beauty in Christianity that does not exist in Islam. There are a number of contemporary musicians who converted from Islam to Christianity. Their works can be heard online and on various radio stations.

Medical ministries continue to go forward in Muslim lands as well. There is one reliable story of a Christian medical group that went to an Arab village known to be a very conservative Islamic town. In many such villages no one would dare come to a Christian-sponsored clinic. Nonetheless, when the medical team got there, they saw a long line of people waiting at the clinic door. One after another came in.

"What is the problem? Where does it hurt?"

"No, I'm having no pain, but since you are a Christian group, I hoped you might have a Bible for me."

We know that there are tens of thousands of Muslims coming to Christ each year. Al Jazeera, the principal Arabic language news station, announced that there were millions of North Africans who had become Christians in recent years. No doubt they inflated the numbers in order to incite their listeners, but the claim has some basis in fact.

It is never easy for someone to leave Islam and become a Christian. The shame it causes the family makes it difficult to declare one's faith openly. And when Muslims do become Christians, they often find that the Christians they know do not welcome them—given tribal, ethnic, or social differences. I know of one Sudanese man who became a Christian and was baptized into the church, but later that very church refused to help or protect him. Another man was baptized into a church, but was not permitted to marry a daughter of the congregation who was of a different social and ethnic class. Certainly these kinds of things have happened in the West too, but for new believers from Muslim countries they can be devastating.

Many Muslims also come to Christ because of dreams. In the West we think of dreams as a kind of garbage can of the subconscious, and we don't ascribe much importance to them. In the East, however, dreams are very meaningful. For example, if the patriarch Joseph appears to you in a dream when your wife is pregnant, you should name your child Joseph, and you can be confident that he, like Joseph, will be handsome and wise.

Religious bookstands throughout the Middle East always seem to have books on four subjects: sex, the last days, evil spirits (jinni), and dreams. Many people—women in particular—get together daily to talk to one another about the dreams they had the previous night. They then help one another interpret the dreams. Some see a figure in their dreams they recognize as Jesus, and so they seek out a Christian woman who can tell them about him. Others see a cross in the sky and recognize it as a Christian sign. Still others attend Christian meetings, where they are delivered from demonic possession.

One Muslim man was riding a bus on his way back from the hajj in Mecca. He had been frustrated throughout the hajj and didn't feel that he was changed at all by what should have been an ultimate religious experience. In fact, if anything, he felt worse. He got on the bus and exchanged pleasantries with the driver. When he mentioned his frustration, the driver asked, "Have you tried Jesus?" The man didn't respond; he rode the bus, got off, and went home. When he returned to his own country, he looked up someone he thought was a Christian and asked him for some materials on Christianity. He was given, among other things, a DVD. He played the DVD, and the first person he saw on it was the bus driver.

Such things seem, and undoubtedly are, strange to Western ears. But God did move through visions, healings, and miracles in biblical times, and he may well be doing so now. The West is so dominated by scientific rationalism that we can barely conceive of this kind of divine action anymore, but in the East it is a reality.

Another Arab man had a sick wife. He hoped for her healing and took her to various doctors, but had no success. In a dream, he got a phone number. He wrote it down and went back to bed. The next morning when he awoke, he found the phone number he had written down and thought he would give it a try. He called, and the person on the other end didn't identify himself, but asked him why he called. The man said he didn't really know whether this was a live phone number or not, but wanted to try it, since he received it in a dream. The number in fact turned out to be a Christian ministry. He brought his ailing wife to the ministry, where she was cured through intercessory prayer.

When talking with Muslims about Christianity I refuse to critique the Prophet: I may as well tell a Catholic that Mary was a loose woman. For fourteen centuries Muhammad has been lifted up as the perfect role model for Muslims. Attacking or even questioning Muhammad only raises the ire of Muslims. Rather, I like to talk with Muslims about the love of God. For Muslims, Allah is an austere lawgiver, and the Prophet warns of doom for the disobedient. The Christian God, on the other hand, is a loving Father, and it was God's love for us that caused him to send his Son to redeem us and remove our shame. A perceptive Muslim will soon recognize that neither Allah nor Muhammad showed such love, but to make this point it is hardly necessary to denigrate the Prophet Muhammad.

In light of this, I sometimes use the admittedly corny illustration of an orange to describe God's love.

"What is this?" I ask.

"An orange," comes the reply.

"What color is it?"

"Orange."

"What is this part?" I ask, pointing to the surface.

"An orange peel," the person answers.

"What about this one?"

"A piece of orange."

"What happens if you squeeze the orange?"

"You get orange juice."

"God is like that. His nature is love; his name is love; he is made of love. All the parts of him are love. If you taste him, you will taste love; if you get to know any part of him, you will find love."

The people are usually delighted to hear this, since their own families, fathers, and God usually don't show such love.

I know of one Saudi woman who became Christian and then shared her faith with other women acquaintances. When her father learned of it, he cut out her tongue and then killed her. Her tongue was the appropriate organ to cut out since she was a poet, but her death did not stop her words from going out. Her Christian poetry in Arabic is still available today. Though her father committed a ghastly crime, he was not prosecuted for it because his friends and neighbors approved of the killing. It would have been a greater dishonor for the father to let the shameful Christian stain grow than it was to erase it by murder. These "honor killings" remove the source of the dishonor and are rarely brought to court.

Sadly, such honor killings of Christian converts are not uncommon. In the East, shame is a stronger principle than justice. If a Muslim child converts to Christianity, the family will see the child as a source of shame. Conversion is not merely a change of religious affiliation as it would be in the West, but a rejection of the family itself. The child is not seen as an individual who can choose what to believe, but as one small part of a large family and community with a common tradition, ancestry, and religion. By converting to another religion, the young person denies the nation, kin, and culture, in addition to the common religion. To the father, it is as if the beautiful body of Arab Muslim society suddenly developed an enormous and ugly mole on its face. Such a flagrant obscenity cannot be permitted; it must be removed. In my own extended family, for example, I am still a pariah.

I know of a young Jordanian woman who was married with two children. After her conversion she was stoned to death by her Muslim father, even though her husband was also a Christian. The husband could not protect her.

In Islam, all is one, and one is all. In the West, different aspects of our lives peaceably coexist. For instance, a man could have a Christian daughter who works in a family business and supports the same football team as her father. If she decided one day to take a job with another company, she would still be the man's Christian daughter and fellow sports fan. Not so in Islam; Islamic society does not separate life into independent spheres.

As a rule, Muslim men want to argue about points of faith and politics, whereas Muslim women want to know more about the social life of Christians. When I meet with Muslim men, they ask about the logic of the Trinity and the need for four Gospels. They want to argue about the politics of the Western/Christian nations and so on. These questions are almost programmed into them: Muslim men have been asking these questions of Christians for centuries. Women, on the other hand, want to know, for example, what marriage is like in Christianity. Is it true that a man can have only one wife? Do Christian men beat their wives? How many times a day must a Christian pray?

Sadly, most Muslim women simply accept their subordinate status as being Allah's will. "This is the portion that Allah has allotted me" is their refrain. But many Muslim women are becoming Christian. In fact, Muslim women are becoming Christian at a greater rate than are men. They find Christianity liberating in more than one way.

Though Arabs officially profess hatred for the West and believe it deserves to be overthrown, most are simultaneously envious of its wealth and freedoms. If given a chance, most would get on a plane tomorrow for the United States or Europe. This kind of ambivalence makes conversations about Christianity difficult. I generally have to sift through a lot of social and political issues that stand in the way of a Muslim coming to know Christ.

Islam also often manages to shoot itself in the foot, creating openings for Christian evangelism. For example, some years back, when women were beginning to enter Arab workplaces, a devout Muslim woman asked her imam how she could remain in an office space with a male who was not her relative, a situation that was becoming increasingly common. The imam bumped her question up the Islamic ladder to a higher-ranking imam. After considerable deliberation, the latter issued a fatwa, which said, in effect,

> The problem is that the man and the woman are not related, and therefore cannot be together under the same roof. How then can they become related? If a woman breastfeeds someone, that person takes her bodily fluids into himself, thus effectively becoming a child of the woman. So what you must do is to nurse the man with whom you are working. He will then be your relative, and you will have obeyed Allah.[5]

As anyone could guess, this fatwa was received with astonished disbelief. The woman reported the nature of the fatwa to others, and it became international news in the Muslim world.[6] How on earth could someone in the twentieth century come up with something that was so patently ridiculous? And coming from a high-ranking imam from the largely misogynist Arab world, it sounded almost pornographic. This naturally led to questioning: Can the fourteen-hundred-year-old words of the Prophet really guide the life of a nation in the twenty-first century?

Another Muslim man from Iran went on the hajj. Farsi was his native tongue, and he spoke only a bit of Arabic. En route, another Arab pilgrim told him there was no way his worship of Allah would be acceptable with such poor Arabic. The man decided that if Allah would not accept his Arabic, he would no longer accept Allah either.

Previously, Arabs thought that only the poor and the idiots became Christians. Now, more people who are clearly sane and solvent are becoming Christian. My sister recently told me that there are now three or four "Crazies" (Christians) on our old street alone. I'd like to meet them, but if I were caught near my old home and mosque, I'd likely be killed.[7]

Unfortunately, the relationship between many ancient Christian groups and Muslims in the Middle East is not friendly. The Copts, for example, have been oppressed by the Muslims for centuries, so they would much rather see the Muslims overthrown than converted. Even evangelical Christians in the Middle East are sometimes less than evangelistic. An evangelical Arab pastor once told me, "As far as I'm concerned, the Muslims can go to hell. We've got enough Christians to worry about." People who resent and even hate Muslims are hardly likely to present the love of Christ to them. I certainly understand how many Arab Christians got to this point, but I hope they can come to see their Muslim neighbors through the eyes of Christ.

CHAPTER SIXTEEN

CURRENT MINISTRY

I t is no longer possible for missionaries to go openly to Muslim nations, as did Samuel Zwemer and others in the 1800s and early 1900s. Nonetheless, there are many Western Christians in Muslim lands who do evangelism as bivocational missionaries. Frankly, there are few of them who are effective as evangelists. I know of only about a dozen who are truly fluent in Arabic, and Westerners face enormous cultural and social barriers when in Arab lands. Many Arab Christians will tell you that they don't want Western missionaries, at least in the role of evangelists or church planters. What they often need are pastoral counselors and teachers for Muslim converts who struggle to live out their faith in very tough circumstances.

Most Westerners have difficulty being learners. When they get to the Global South they immediately want to provide leadership. They seem to ignore the fact that Arabs have been leading their own societies for centuries, often more successfully than the Westerners who colonized the Middle East and North Africa.

A fascinating recent missionary trend is the placement of Latinos in the Middle East as bivocational missionaries. Latinos have advantages over most Westerners in these roles. Since the Arabs controlled Spain for nearly seven centuries, the Spanish culture is far closer to that of Arabia than are those of Western Europe or the United States. Latinos are instinctively more attuned to the social practices of the Arabs; they look more like Arabs, and they have dinner late and stay up late. They love to joke around, are hardly fixated on the clock, and are often content with modest housing. It is ironic but no doubt providential that the people who were conquered by the Arabs in the 700s CE are now presenting Christ to the Arabs in the twenty-first century.

My theological education in the United States also continues to bear fruit in Muslim evangelism. Many intellectual challenges in the history of Islam are still pressing today. For instance, in the fourteenth century a rational school of Islam (Matazalites) argued that the Qur'an was created, not coeternal with Allah. They lost the scholarly battle, and the official teaching of Islam remains that the Qur'an is coeternal with Allah.

This may sound like an obscure issue, but it is still significant when relating to educated Muslims. If the Qur'an is coeternal with Allah, how can Allah be the only one, with nothing at all beside him? And if the Qur'an is eternal, it must also be at once perfect, inerrant, and immutable. But if it is eternal, inerrant, and immutable, then one passage cannot be more eternal, inerrant, or immutable than any other. Nonetheless, the Qur'an itself states that a later text can supersede and even abrogate an earlier one.[1] But this is a logical problem. Why should some Qur'anic texts abrogate earlier texts if the entire Qur'an is one eternally created whole? My seminary training in hermeneutics helped me understand this problem. In contrast, the Bible is recognized as a book of progressive revelation.

We know that what happened early on in redemptive history is shaped and fulfilled by later passages.

Unfortunately, many Muslims who turn to Christ don't know who they can trust. It is not uncommon for churches and even home study groups to be infiltrated by secret police or security forces. One church thought it would test each member to see if they were Christian. Their test? Eat pork. Anyone who would break this clear rule of Islam must truly be a Christian. How sad that they had to devise this test. It is sad that Christians in Muslim countries must constantly hide in fear, and also sad that they would feel it necessary to resort to a gimmick to feel safe.

The first time I went back to a Muslim country after living in the United States, I spent a night in a hotel. At five in the morning I heard the clear call of the muezzin:

God is greater,
There is no god but Allah
I testify that Muhammad is the messenger of Allah
Hasten to prayer, Hasten to prosperity
Prayer is better than sleep
God is greater
There is no god but Allah.

I rose and knelt by the side of my bed. Then it occurred to me— you're no longer a Muslim, you haven't been for over twenty years, and you don't need to pray to the Muslim's Allah. But the urge was powerful. I had been accustomed to performing this ritual throughout my entire childhood and young adulthood. Islam soaks into the fabric of every Arab's identity, and its tint remains even years after a person has converted.

Some years ago it was necessary for us to move back to the United States in order to help care for Belinda's failing parents. We all found that move to be a culture shock.

But now, some years later, our children are adults, and Belinda's parents have gone to their reward. So the work that began back in Cairo continues throughout the globe. At present Belinda and I spend half the year in Michigan and half in Spain. Of course that doesn't mean that we are only in those two places, but our travels begin from one of those home bases.

I speak at conferences for Muslims and to missionaries to Muslims. I work with some people in media to reach Arabic speakers. I am in communication with people all over the world who are Muslim converts and Christian workers. I am consulted on questions of doctrine, church practices, family relations, and business. I often raise funds for various ministries and needs. Thankfully, a new generation is taking up the tasks that I have been performing.

For example, one young refugee became a convert at one of our presentations in the Netherlands. Since he looked even younger than he was, he had told the Dutch authorities that he was a minor so he would be able to stay in the Netherlands. After being discipled by us for a short time, he became convicted of the need to be honest as a Christian. He dutifully went back to the Dutch authorities and told them that he was an adult, even when he had originally applied for asylum. He was deported back to his country of origin.

Shortly after his arrival there he was jailed for reasons related to his new faith. He spent six months in jail, in deplorable conditions. But in that time, he never gave up on Christ, nor did Christ give up on him. In fact, his faith grew by leaps and bounds. This young man was able to find his way back to the Netherlands, legally, and is now one of the primary leaders in the Dutch Arabic-speaking churches.

A young Christian woman from Iraq left her husband to flee to Europe with her child. She had to pass through Greece on her way. While in Greece she witnessed to Christ. En route to the Netherlands, she also witnessed to Christ. And in the Netherlands she likewise witnessed to Christ. In the Netherlands she planted two churches among Arab speakers. And she is still going strong. She just can't keep quiet about Christ.

Her husband was finally able to join her in the Netherlands. In him she found her biggest evangelistic challenge. It took seven long years till he received Christ. They too are now important leaders in the Arabic-speaking churches in Europe.

My own work is both to encourage these younger Christians and to keep evangelizing among the thousands of Arab refugees now in Europe. I see the movement of Arabs into Europe as a historical moment for the Christian faith. Never before have so many Muslims been accessible to Christ. Whereas their governments in Iraq, Syria, or the Gulf might have made it nearly impossible to be openly Christian, their new lives in Europe make it quite possible. Though the largely secular nations of Europe are not keen on evangelizing, they do permit freedom of religious choice. So when we enter Arabic-speaking refugee camps or neighborhoods, we do not advertise our intentions with the government. If an authority at one of the camps does not want us to enter, we obey. But often, one of the Arab refugees will offer us hospitality and invite us into their camp. We Arabs highly value hospitality, and the poor refugees are often eager to talk to someone in Arabic who cares about their situation.

Many are open to hearing about Christ, who has turned out to be their only hope. Islam is the reason that most of them are displaced. They are fleeing their fellow Muslims. Many have seen death firsthand. They have lost family members and neighbors because they are not part of the Islamic State. They have seen beheadings on YouTube. They have heard radical Islamists brag about their cruelty to other Muslims. They have heard the calls to strike terror into the hearts of the Westerners by bloody and fatal bombings.

All of this has left many decent, normal Muslims disgusted with and despondent over their faith. In the United States, I know that many of us are embarrassed by the behavior of pastors or priests involved in sexual scandals. But you would have to multiply that embarrassment by a factor of thousands to understand the feelings of Muslims who see their fellow believers murder, rape, and destroy on a daily basis, and then brag about it.

In addition to the evangelistic work among Muslims in Europe, we also provide support for those who have become Christian. We have established a small center in Spain to which we invite Muslim converts from North Africa, the Middle East, and Europe. The center serves as a retreat and training ground. There we hold classes and discussions on topics like family life as a Christian or the reality of persecution. In addition, we teach some basic courses on the Bible and Christian beliefs. I teach some of these courses, but most are taught by others who are also Muslim converts.

I do not rejoice over the fact that so many Muslims have been displaced, but I do rejoice over the opportunities this has created. As was true in the early church, persecution scatters believers and makes them evangelists.

EPILOGUE

M any Muslims are coming to know Christ. And I see the current events in the Arab world as leading to further growth in Christianity. The view of Christianity in Egypt and throughout the Arab world has changed dramatically after the Arab Spring. On the one hand, the ugliest portrait of Islam is apparent in country after country. On the other, the beautiful love of Christ beckons all.

Tens of thousands of Muslims are becoming Christians in Europe, and tens of thousands more in the Arab-speaking world. As an example of how things have changed, consider the recent opportunity I had to serve as a trainer for missionaries. A Christian from Egypt, I was training South Korean Christians, in Europe, to work in the Arab world. Clearly the days of the British gentry trekking off to Africa carrying a Bible and wearing a pith helmet have come to an end. The globe is shrinking, and nationalities are blending. Getting involved in God's redemptive mission can take many forms today, from medical missions to media missions, teaching, aid and development, and tent making of various kinds. Where God is already at work, any of these means can be effective.

As mentioned earlier, God sometimes has some pretty dramatic ways of bringing Muslims in. Since Muslims are so dogmatic about their faith, God uses healings, dreams, and other miracles that show his truth backed by his loving power. I call it God's "two-by-four method": if you won't listen to reason, I'll smack you upside the head with miraculous surprises. The Holy Spirit is a powerful weapon in the battle of faiths, one that Islam does not have.

Another reason I believe Christianity will continue to grow in the Muslim world is that global communication is now so easy. On any given day I am in contact with supporters in the United States, recent converts in Libya, our training center in Europe, and a church leader in Indonesia. The Internet is available globally, though the poor may lack direct access to it. Email has overtaken snail mail by factors of millions. North American teenagers send thousands of texts to one another every month, and teens in developing countries are not far behind. Whereas one hundred years ago the news of the gospel had to be delivered in person, today it can be delivered in multiple ways. Today you have to live in a pretty thick cocoon not to hear at least something of Christ.

As for me, I have no regrets about following Christ, though many people have asked whether I do. After all, I had to flee my native country and leave behind a society, family, and language that I know and love. I gave up some measure of wealth. Today when I travel to the Middle East and North Africa I still risk possible death. If I were to return to my family home in Egypt under my true Egyptian name, I would likely be imprisoned, or perhaps even killed.

But I do not regret it. Not once in the years since I became a Christian have I felt that I made a mistake. The love of Christ found me, and I will not leave him. I first saw this love in the meeting of the students in Cairo. I then saw it in churches in the United States and in Europe. In fact, I have seen it on the six continents that I have visited or lived in. And it all starts with the one who showed us love: "Greater love has no one than this: to lay down one's life for one's friends," said Jesus (John 15:13). I have experienced this love for over thirty years as a Christian and have not questioned whether I should follow Christ since that first day in Cairo. On the other hand, I saw—and continue to see—the political anger, religious insecurity, and destructive sexism that Islam has produced. I have seen the violence of Muslim versus Christian and Muslim versus Muslim. Islamists are eager to die for their religion, whereas the leader of Christianity died for us. The difference is clear: Islam is submission to an impersonal lawgiver who honors his fallen warriors, whereas Christianity honors those who follow the personal and living God of love. In Christianity, heaven came down to us. In Islam, we must get to heaven by our good deeds or by martyrdom.

The New Testament book of Hebrews also convinces me that I have followed the truth. It begins by acknowledging that God did reveal himself in many ways. Then, however, it goes on to show us how the revelation of God in Jesus Christ was the greatest of all God's self-revelations:

> In the past God spoke to our ancestors through the prophets at many times and in various ways, but in these last days he has spoken to us by his Son, whom he appointed heir of all things, and through whom also he made the universe. The Son is the radiance of God's glory and the exact representation of his being, sustaining all things by his powerful word.

After he had provided purification for sins, he sat down at the
right hand of the Majesty in heaven. (Hebrews 1:1-3)

The prophets God sent knew about God and told his people what
they knew. But Jesus was not only a messenger of God, but God
himself. Jesus not only told his listeners what God was like and
what God demanded, he showed them God himself.

Seeing the real thing makes an enormous difference. For instance,
compare a description of a painting by Michelangelo in the Sistine
Chapel to the painting itself. Even if the description was very good,
it would be nothing in comparison to seeing the actual painting. Or
compare my description of my spouse to the woman herself. Again,
I might provide a lengthy and accurate description, but the
knowledge I could give you would be nothing in comparison to
actually meeting and knowing her. This is true to an infinite degree
of the revelation of God in Christ. God is far beyond all telling,
even by inspired prophets. Jesus is the God who actually came to
us, and "we have seen his glory, the glory of the one and only Son,
who came from the Father, full of grace and truth" (John 1:14).

The book of Hebrews explains how Jesus was superior to any of
the other prophets who warned the people, and I believe this includes the last prophet—Muhammad. Jesus is superior even to
Moses since he was not only God's Prophet but also Priest and
King. Jesus is superior to any of the high priests because he did not
have to first make atonement for his own sins before he sacrificed
for the people. Jesus is superior to Joshua since Jesus delivers the
people into the true place of rest. And finally, Jesus is superior to
Abraham, even though Abraham is the father of Jews, Christians,
and Muslims. The writer of Hebrews shows this by pointing to
Melchizedek, the "king of Salem and priest of God Most High"

(Hebrews 7:1). Abraham, who is the father of Israel and the Jews, the father of Ishmael and the Muslims, and the father of Christians, gave his offerings to Melchizedek. Melchizedek, it is said, had no ancestry, no father, no mother, and was without beginning or end, like the Son of God (Hebrews 7:3). Jesus was that Son of God, to whom all the children of Abraham must offer themselves. The life that Jesus lived is the life he gives to us. In his life we find the obedience and forgiveness that reconciles us to God.

Muslims do believe that Jesus was one in the line of Allah's prophets, which included Noah, Moses, and David. But for Muslims, Muhammad is the final and true prophet, the one who restored true monotheism to the children of Abraham.[1] Nonetheless, Muhammad was not God himself; he, like all the other prophets, only heard from God and then died as a man.

There is, in my judgment, no comparison between Muhammad and Jesus. Christ is superior to all priests and prophets, including Muhammad. Muhammad called Allah the "merciful and compassionate." Yet his visions and practices show God to be a distant master and vindictive king. Muhammad demanded complete obedience from his followers and killed many who would not submit to his rule. On the other hand, Jesus said, "love your enemies and pray for those who persecute you, that you may be children of your Father in heaven" (Matthew 5:44-45). Christ was obedient to God his Father and permitted himself to be killed by his enemies. This self-sacrifice is exactly what Muslims saw Christians doing during the revolutions in Egypt. As one Muslim wrote: "The Brotherhood may have weapons and bombs, but watch those Christians; in two days they prayed, and the President was toppled."

Muhammad is called the Warner, the one who warns his followers of the judgment to come and calls them to submit to Allah.

Though Allah is called "the compassionate, the merciful," Muslims cannot be sure that they have received God's mercy or that they will be received with compassion in paradise. There is no certainty of salvation in Islam, unless you die as a martyr for the faith. At the end of time Allah will weigh the books that the angels have placed on your scale. If the Book of the Sins weighs more heavily than the Book of Good Deeds, there is only punishment. Forgiveness and restoration are never certain.

As I mentioned earlier, more Muslims have come to Christ in the last forty years than have done so in the previous fourteen centuries. Most of them come to Christ for the same reason that I did: they see the love of Christ and of Christians. My task is to support them. I do this today by discipling new believers at our study center, visiting oppressed believers throughout the Arab world, writing, and raising money for converts who have lost most or all of their family and social connections.

I am confident that when my days on earth come to an end, I will not stand before a God who merely looks at the scale weighing my good deeds versus my evil ones. Were it so, I would live in uncertainty, as many Muslims do. I know that it is not what we can do for God that matters, but what God in Christ has done for us. I am not interested in the wine, milk, honey, or maidens of an Islamic paradise. I am confident, rather, that I will live in an eternal relationship with my loving Father, who has shown his love by sending his Son. I am also confident that when I come face to face with God I will be joined by people from every tongue and nation. Many of them will be Arabs who bow before Christ and confess him as Lord. It will be a great delight to see them—and to know that I was able to introduce some of them to Christ.

AFTERWORD

Kent Van Til

Y ou have now heard Stephen's story.
I suspect that there were surprises for you, as there were for me. In particular, you may have been surprised to learn that this is a time of great harvest among Muslims.

At the conclusion of this work, I asked Stephen: "What would you like English-speaking readers to take away from this story?" He had a few answers for me.

1. Don't lump all Muslims in one pile, especially if that pile is filled with hatred and violence. The vast majority of Muslims do not support terrorists groups who act in the name of Islam. There is a great variety among Muslims, just as there is among Christians.

2. Be aware of the struggle that Muslim-background believers are facing. Pray for them. Their lives in the Middle East have never been easy, and their new lives in Europe are challenging as well.

3. Be active in the support of global human rights. It is not right that new Christians should lose jobs, family, or citizenship

because they have left Islam, or that women should inherit only half of what men do, and so on.

4. Support humanitarian efforts for Arab refugees. There have not been this many refugees in Europe since WWII. Their presence in Europe is a great challenge, but also a great opportunity.

5. Recognize that persecution is a natural part of Christian faith. The fact that we have not seen it recently in the West is unusual, not the norm.

I also asked Stephen what, if anything, Westerners might do in ministry in the Middle East. Here's his response to that query:

1. There are many restricted-access countries where the gospel of Christ is hardly known, such as the Gulf States. Since the few Christians in those lands are largely in hiding, it is still necessary to introduce people to Christ for the first time. The only way Westerners can enter these nations is to be bivocational ambassadors for Christ. So, for example, for decades Filipina housekeepers have worked in the Gulf States. While in that role they have often had opportunity to witness to the families they work for. Other roles such as doctors, engineers, business managers, professors, and the like are needed in those states, and Christians can be frontline evangelists as such.

2. Most of the predominantly Muslim countries in the world now have at least a few churches. But these churches are typically small and struggling. Since Western Christians typically have long years of experience in their churches, they also have great experience in being Christian spouses, businesspeople, parents, deacons, and so on. So there is much need for people to come alongside the existing churches and disciple the newer believers, showing them that Christianity is not merely a one-time

decision but a lifelong process in which all aspects of life are guided by the Spirit of Christ.

- Keep in mind that such a missionary may also need to be bivocational to enter many Muslim lands.
- Keep in mind also that such work may require near mastery of Arabic or another language.
- Keep in mind too that Westerners do not have all the answers for Easterners. What Westerners do have is more experience and resources. We have been involved in Christian families, businesses, and churches for generations, and might have useful models for those who are new to the faith.

3. More and more well-educated Muslims are coming to Christ. They will not be satisfied with facile Sunday school answers to their difficult questions and life issues. Some Westerners will need to work with these people at their own intellectual level, and preferably in their own language.

4. Pray. Anyone, regardless of language or financial ability, can pray, and that is the most important work. "Our struggle is not against flesh and blood, but against the rulers, against the authorities, against the powers of this dark world" (Ephesians 6:12). There is certainly a spiritual struggle going on in Arab lands. It often plays out in political and physical ways. For example, Mesopotamia, which is current-day Iraq, has been characterized by violence for millennia. It is hard not to believe that a spirit of violence has been dominant in that region. Pray for the overthrow of that spirit, and its replacement with the spirit of Christ's peace.

DISCUSSION
QUESTIONS

CHAPTER 1: A KID IN CAIRO

1. How did Stephen's parents' religious practices influence him growing up?

2. What is the significance of the pilgrimage to Mecca? What similarities and differences do you see between the hajj and Christian practices?

3. How do Muslims relate to tradition? How is this similar to or different from how Christians understand tradition?

4. How did the death of Stephen's father and cousin affect him? Have you ever experienced such losses?

5. What kinds of questions might you have for God in the midst of this kind of emotional turmoil?

CHAPTER 2: ADOLESCENCE IN AN ARAB FAMILY

1. What factors contributed to Stephen's suicide attempt? Does this raise any emotions or issues for you?

2. How do you respond to the marriage practices of Middle Eastern cultures? How do they differ from Western practices?

3. What are the historical roots of the practice of dowry? What cultural assumptions might be embedded in it?

4. What would it be like to have to follow a strict set of rules for dating and social life as a direct result of religious and cultural practices? What similarities or contrasts do you see here between Islam and Christianity regarding these practices?

CHAPTER 3: ENCOUNTERING CHRIST

1. What is most striking to you about Stephen's account of being part of the Muslim Brotherhood?

2. How do you respond to the quote "Islam is perfect, though its practice is often flawed"?

3. Stephen reports that young Arab men say, "Have some fun with the Christian girls before marriage, and then marry a good Muslim woman." What does this suggest about how Christians are viewed in other parts of the world?

4. Why is the notion of God as love a strange idea to Muslims?

5. Stephen contrasts Islam and Christianity in terms of praying as a trembling servant versus praying as a child to Baba. What does this say about the relationship one has as a Christian believer in God? Is it easy for a person to have faith when not trying to be intimately connected to God?

6. Death was Stephen's likely fate if he converted. Have you ever felt like your life would be ruined by being a Christian? What are the risks and costs of following Jesus?

7. What is instructive about how Stephen became a Christian? What does his experience suggest about how Christians might engage in outreach and mission?

CHAPTER 4: A FRIGHTENED NEW CHRISTIAN

1. What might it have felt like for Stephen to have been baptized and (1) outwardly celebrate his faith or (2) hide it for fear of his life?
2. Under what circumstances might Christians conceal their faith?
3. How might facing persecution shape your practice of the faith?
4. How might Stephen's character resemble that of a martyr?
5. What might Western Christians learn from how Stephen quite literally left everything to follow Christ?
6. Do we see people today who are willing to surrender and sacrifice everything at a moment's notice to follow Christ? What might that look like for you?

CHAPTER 5: IN THE UNITED STATES

1. What kinds of culture shock did Stephen experience when he came to America?
2. What might Stephen's mother have experienced in losing her son to Christianity? Are there parallels in Stephen's mother continuing to love him as Christ does us?
3. How do you feel about the way relationships are approached when finding a spouse among Arabs?
4. How did Stephen's education pay off in his US ministry?
5. How does being poor and facing poverty speak to being devoted to Christ?
6. Would leaving everything to better your life and then facing new troubles and difficulties cause turmoil in your newfound faith? Would it strengthen your faith?

CHAPTER 6: MINISTRY IN THE UNITED STATES

1. Dearborn, Michigan, has the largest percentage population of Arabs in all of the United States. Does this surprise you? How should Christians respond?

2. How do you deal with Muslim differences, especially when it comes to sharing the gospel in the United States?

3. What can we learn from the man in the park who accepted Jesus in such a simple way through respect and the observation of Christian character?

4. What do you imagine Stephen's reunion with his mother was like? Does his ministry seem to have any effect on his relationship with her? How would this affect him?

CHAPTER 7: ARABS AND THE WEST

1. In response to dealing with race post-9/11, do you think the actions against Muslims were fair, or is it racial profiling?

2. What does it feel like to read about the way Muslims view the West?

3. "The gospel has rarely gone out to friends of Christ; far more often it has been presented to his enemies." How do you respond to this statement?

4. Do Western Christians invest enough in other cultures and religions? Or is the United States rightly judged as being ignorant of Islam and other cultures?

5. After reading this chapter, how would you describe the relationship between Islam and the Christian West? What might Westerners be missing?

CHAPTER 8: IN EUROPE

1. What would it be like to not be able to raise questions about your faith in your homeland?

2. What is your response when reading how ethnic differences trump religious unity?

3. How is demonstrating Christ's love and not challenging others' faith counter to Western tendencies?

4. Stephen says, "God uses antiheroes like Khomeini and Ahmadinejad to spread the gospel as much as he uses Christian missionaries." What is your reaction to this? What is your view of missionaries?

5. How do you relate to those around you who do not accept Christ but do accept or respect you? How do you maintain those relationships? Is it a challenge?

6. One Muslim convert to Christianity clearly had been led to Christ before meeting Stephen. How do you think the Holy Spirit works in such cases?

CHAPTER 9: MISUNDERSTANDINGS IN EUROPE

1. Think back to your first reaction to the Christian faith. Was it moving and as strong as these stories?

2. As an outsider visiting Saudi Arabia, how would you feel to know that the government does not allow churches there?

3. In response to cartoonists dishonoring Muhammad, Stephen asks, "How would Christians feel if Muslims depicted Jesus as a pedophile or a sorcerer?" How do you respond?

4. What are your reactions to dhimmitude and sharia law?

5. Why is it so difficult for Westerners to accept that there are such things as dhimmitude and apostasy in the twenty-first century? What clouds our worldview?

6. Stephen mentions a Muslim man who converted to Christianity and then asked how many times a day he should beat his wife. Stephen then asks, "How do you reconcile the religious-cultural practices of Islam with the laws and customs of the West?" What is your response?

CHAPTER 10: CHRISTIANS IN EGYPT

1. What are your views on the treatment of women in Islam?

2. Stephen persecuted a Coptic child in grade school, and sees abuse and shame used often at such an early age. How are we socialized into our religious practices? Do we shame and abuse those who are different from us?

3. If you were a Coptic Christian in Egypt, what do you think you would do to survive?

4. Are there any laws that you know of in the United States that discriminate against certain religions or religious practices? Does that seem hypocritical or ethical in the eyes of the law?

5. Egypt was once the center of Christianity. What questions does this raise in your mind?

CHAPTER 11: ISRAEL AND THE MUSLIMS

1. Muslims interpret the Qur'an with a wooden literalism. How does this compare to Christians and the Bible? Should we interpret God's Word literally?

2. What happens when someone understands for the first time the direct access he or she has to God?

3. What cultural barriers hinder the belief that we can be fully accepted by God and fully sinners at the same time?

4. Children in Palestine are brought up to know that they will die in support of their country. What do you think about this? Is dying for your country considered martyrdom in the West?

5. Have you experienced unity in Christ among people who had previously opposed each other? What was that like?

6. Do you think achieving peace in the Middle East is realistic? Why or why not? How can we achieve this?

CHAPTER 12 : MARRIAGE AND FAMILY IN ISLAM

1. Stephen finally returned to Cairo after many years of absence. However, he had to stay far from his childhood home so no one would recognize him. How do you imagine this would make you feel if you had to do the same?

2. Westerners believe female circumcision is sexual abuse. Muslims see it as a necessary religious and cultural practice. How could you convince them to change this practice?

3. Would Christians today accept the marriage of a nine-year-old girl and a fifty-year-old man? What biblical or theological reasons make this unacceptable?

4. "When Muslim women convert to Christianity they face great hardships. They could lose their children, their alimony, and their inheritance—in other words, everything." What makes this statement so shocking?

CHAPTER 13 : CHRISTIAN–MUSLIM FAMILIES

1. What do you think of the justification for not having adoption in Islam?

2. In the Muslim world no one adopts children even though the children may end up living on the street. In contrast, what has been the Christian response to orphaned or abandoned children?

3. Do you think the horrible sexual practices that Stephen describes (e.g., the father and brother who raped their daughter/sister) are normal in Islam, or do they come from a more radical and warped interpretation of religious ideology?

4. Do you see anything in Muslim sexual ethics and practice in a positive light? If so, what?

CHAPTER 14: EGYPT NOW

1. The Egyptian secret police personally burned down their headquarters to destroy documentation of their actions. If you were in such a situation, would you trust the government and feel safe? What does this say about how authority is implemented in Islam?

2. It is interesting that Gamal Abdel Nasser's prose is equated with Martin Luther King Jr.'s or Winston Churchill's. Are you surprised that there is such a thing as a progressive Arab? Why?

3. The Muslim Brotherhood is known to have contributed some good to society by helping the poor and building schools, hospitals, and factories. How do these actions fit with their desire to establish an Islamic state?

4. When groups like the Muslim Brotherhood or Egyptian Islamic Jihad are in power, those who challenge their worldview are imprisoned or killed. Is this justifiable? How should we respond to those who challenge our worldview?

5. After centuries of Christian persecution, what would it be like to see a Coptic priest and Muslim imam walk arm in arm to protest the king's misuse of power?

6. The Muslim Brotherhood persecuted Christians and Egyptians who did not follow the Brotherhood's ideology. Why do you think there is still this type of violence and abuse in the twenty-first century?

CHAPTER 15: MUSLIM CONVERTS

1. How would it feel to know that even your extended family would be put in harm's way by your conversion to Christianity and would continue to be persecuted long after your absence? Knowing this, could you go all in with your faith? How do you overcome these obstacles when it comes to following Christ?

2. Could you keep your faith a secret if you were in a foreign land where Christianity is not accepted and your life (or your family's) could be threatened?

3. What is your reaction to the example of the father cutting out his own daughter's tongue?

4. Stephen explains that "Islamic society does not separate life into independent spheres." How does this compare to life in the West?

5. Stephen outlined three reasons for Berber missional success. Could these reasons be true for missions in general?

6. "Can the fourteen-hundred-year-old words of the Prophet really guide the life of a nation in the twenty-first century?" What are your thoughts on this? Does the West face similar questions?

CHAPTER 16 : CURRENT MINISTRY

1. Have we listened to Arab Christians when we are told they do not want Western missionaries? Why might they feel this way?

2. "Most Westerners have difficulty being learners. When they get to the Global South they immediately want to provide leadership." Do you think this claim is true? Why or why not?

3. Do the Christians of the West have a "Savior complex" when it comes to missions? Explain.

4. Stephen recounts the story of the young refugee who converted to Christianity in the Netherlands. He was deported to his homeland, where he spent time in jail—and his faith grew. Have you heard similar stories about someone in jail experiencing growth in their faith? If so, tell the group.

5. What is most inspiring about the stories of converts and their radical dependence on Christ?

6. The last line of the chapter says, "As was true in the early church, persecution scatters believers and makes them evangelists." What opportunities does this create for believers and nonbelievers alike?

NOTES

1 A Kid in Cairo

[1] The minaret is a tower on the mosque from which the muezzin, a professional crier, calls the faithful to prayer.

[2] The Alawites of Syria are one clear and current example of this.

[3] Anas ibn Malik reported the Messenger of God as saying, "A man's prayer in his house is equivalent to a single observance of prayer, his prayer in a tribal mosque is worth twenty-five, his prayer in a Friday mosque is equivalent to fifty thousand, his prayer in my mosque (in Medina) is also equivalent to fifty thousand, and his prayer in the Sacred Mosque [that is, the Haram at Mecca] is equivalent to a hundred thousand." Ibn Maja has transmitted this report (Baghawi, *Mishkat al-Masabih* 4.8.3).

[4] A sura is a chapter or section of the Qur'an, which has 114 suras. All quotations from the Qur'an are taken from Yusuf Ali's translation. See Abdullah Yusufali, "The Meanings of the Holy Qur'an," Islam 101, accessed February 8, 2017, www.islam101.com/quran/yusufAli.

[5] The phrase is: "It is as if your mother has just given you birth."

[6] Qur'an sura 37:99-109. The text refers to Abraham's son without naming him.

[7] This no doubt derives from the extreme heat in Arabia at the time of Muhammad. A corpse of more than a day old would likely explode.

[8] Good deeds are measured on the right shoulder.

2 Adolescence in an Arab Family

[1] Temporomandibular joint. It has to do with a malfunction of the jaw.

[2] The ancient Orthodox Christian Church of Egypt.

3 ENCOUNTERING CHRIST

[1] Sharia law is derived from the Qur'an and the hadiths (collections of sayings by and about the prophet Muhammad). It is a massive body of law developed over centuries. It differs in some details from country to country. In Egypt most people, including myself, followed the Hanafi school of law.

[2] The Hanbali school believes that no Muslim may be ruled over by an infidel. In Muslim lands, therefore, they demand that any Christian who rises to a high level in government or business be removed from that position.

[3] English interpreters of the Qur'an often seek to make their translations of the Arabic comparable to biblical texts that speak of God as love.

[4] Baba in Arabic is the clear equivalent to Abba in Hebrew.

[5] Allah's Apostle said, "No child is born except on *Al-Fitra* (Islam) and then his parents make him Jewish, Christian or Magian, as an animal produces a perfect young animal." *Hadiths of Bukhari*, vol. 6, bk. 60, no. 298, narrated by Abu Huraira. (Hadiths are officially recorded sayings of the prophet Muhammad. The most highly regarded collection is that of Bukhari.)

[6] Allah's Apostle said, "The blood of a Muslim who confesses that none has the right to be worshipped but Allah and that I am His Apostle, cannot be shed except in three cases: for murder, . . . a married person who commits illegal sexual intercourse, and the one who reverts from Islam (apostate) and leaves the Muslims." *Hadiths of Bukhari*, vol. 9, bk. 83, no. 17, narrated by Abdullah.

[7] Saudi Arabia, Northern Sudan, and Pakistan are probably the three most conservative Muslim nations.

[8] "Allah forgiveth not (the sin of) joining other gods with Him; but He forgiveth whom He pleaseth other sins than this: one who joins other gods with Allah, Hath strayed far, far away (from the right)" (sura 4:166).

4 A FRIGHTENED NEW CHRISTIAN

[1] Approximately 12 percent of Egyptians are Copts.

[2] Some Christian missiologists from the insider movements believe that baptism should be optional for people in these circumstances. I disagree. Jesus ordered us to baptize using the trinitarian formula. And baptism is not merely a set of words but an effective sacrament of initiation into Christ.

[3] "When a Moslem apostatizes from the faith, an exposition thereof is to be laid before him in such a manner that if his apostasy should have arisen from

any religious doubts or scruples, those may be removed. The reason for laying an exposition of the faith before him is that it is possible some doubts or errors may have arisen in his mind, which may be removed by such exposition; and as there are two modes of repelling the sin of apostasy, namely, destruction or Islam, and as Islam is preferable to destruction, the evil is rather to be removed by means of an exposition of the faith; but yet this exposition of the faith is not incumbent (according to what the learned have remarked upon this head), since a call to the faith has already reached the apostate.

"An apostate is to be imprisoned for three days; within which time, if he returns to the faith, it is well; but if not, he must be slain." Burhan al-Din Ali, *The Hedaya*, trans. Charles Hamilton (London, 1791), 2:225, cited in Samuel Zwemer. *The Law of Apostasy in Islam* (London: Marshall Brothers, 1924), 40.

The Hedaya is a standard law textbook from the Hanafi school of law, and forms part of the sharia. Zwemer goes on to cite numerous references confirming the death sentence on apostates and the option of providing the apostate three days to recant.

5 IN THE UNITED STATES

[1]The Prophet said, "Whoever keeps a [pet] dog which is neither a watch dog nor a hunting dog, will get a daily deduction of two Qirat from his good deeds." *Hadiths of Bukhari*, vol. 7, bk. 67, no. 389, narrated by Ibn 'Umar. There are numerous other negative speeches about dogs in the hadiths.

6 MINISTRY IN THE UNITED STATES

[1]The name of this opponent was Muawiyah, the first of the Umayyads. He is still despised by the Shiites. Karbala is still considered a holy site by the Shiites.

[2]There are minority Shiite populations in other countries, such as Syria and Lebanon. The Muslim population worldwide is approximately 85 percent Sunni and 15 percent Shiite.

[3]For Sunnis, *ijtihad* or new interpretation closed in the fourteenth century.

7 ARABS AND THE WEST

[1] *Salaam* is the term for peace in Arabic, but Islam is not derived from the term *salaam*, but *yuslem*, which means "to submit."

[2] Others later followed up on this ministry, and it now exists under a different name.

[3] At the time, Arab World Ministries headquarters were located in London.

8 IN EUROPE

[1] Muslim historians Al-Waqidi and Al-Tabari, for example.

[2] Sura 15:9 says, "Verily we have sent down the Dhikr [Qur'an] and surely we will guard it from corruption."

[3] "*The Satanic Verses*," Wikipedia, accessed February 8, 2017, https://en.wiki pedia.org/wiki/The_Satanic_Verses.

[4] His debates have been recorded, and can be found under his name on YouTube.

9 MISUNDERSTANDINGS IN EUROPE

[1] See Oddbjørn Leirvik, *Images of Jesus in Islam* (London: Continuum, 2010); and Mathias Zahniser, *The Mission and Death of Jesus in Islam and Christianity* (Maryknoll NY: Orbis, 2008).

[2] Recep Tayyip Erdoğan, quoted in "Turkey's Charismatic Pro-Islamic Leader," BBC News, November 4, 2002, http://news.bbc.co.uk/2/hi /europe/2270642.stm.

[3] "Swiss Voters Back Ban on Minarets," BBC News, November 29, 2009, http://news.bbc.co.uk/2/hi/8385069.stm.

[4] Uthman, the third of four "Rightly Guided Caliphs," found and destroyed all variations of the Qur'an except one. That one then became the standard text from which all future copies were made.

[5] Such as the permission Allah gave Muhammad to marry his adopted son's wife (sura 33:37-41).

[6] In fact, pictures of all things that have souls are not permitted. For example, "We were with Masruq at the house of Yasar bin Numair. Masruq saw pictures on his terrace and said, 'I heard Abdullah saying that he heard the Prophet saying, "The people who will receive the severest punishment from Allah will be the picture makers.""' *Hadiths of Bukhari*, vol. 7, bk. 72, no. 834, narrated by Muslim.

[7] Dhim is singular, dhimmi is plural, and dhimmitude is the condition.

[8] See Mark Durie, *The Third Choice: Islam, Dhimmitude and Freedom* (n.p.: Deror Books, 2010).

[9] The first four Rightly Guided Caliphs (rulers) are Abu Bakr, Omar, Uthman, and Ali. All were contemporaries of Muhammad who followed his teachings directly.

[10] "Mapping the Global Muslim Population," Pew Research Center, October 7, 2009, www.pewforum.org/2009/10/07/mapping-the-global-muslim -population.

[11] David Cameron, quoted in "State Multiculturalism Has Failed, Says David Cameron," BBC News, February 5, 2011, www.bbc.com/news/uk-politics -12371994.

[12] See Ayaan Hirsi Ali, *Infidel* (New York: Simon & Schuster, 2007).

10 CHRISTIANS IN EGYPT

[1] Arabs usually don't distinguish between contemporary Israelis and historical Jews.

[2] Alexander was succeeded by the Ptolemies. Cleopatra was the last of these rulers.

11 ISRAEL AND THE MUSLIMS

[1] "Jewish Diaspora," *Wikipedia*, accessed December 22, 2016, https://en.wiki pedia.org/wiki/Jewish_diaspora.

[2] Betty Jane Bailey and J. Martin Bailey, *Who Are the Christians of the Middle East?* (Grand Rapids: Eerdmans, 2010).

[3] Gary Burge, *Jesus and the Land* (Grand Rapids: Baker 2010), 113.

[4] 1948 is known as the year of *Nakba* or "the Catastrophe" for Palestinians.

[5] Sura 17:1; Sahih Muslim (collection of hadith), bk. 1, no. 3909.

[6] See, e.g., Walter Brueggemann, *The Land* (Minneapolis: Augsburg, 2002).

[7] Two examples are Jesus' rejection of Satan's temptation to receive the kingdoms of the world (Matthew 4:8-10) and his rejection of James and John's mother's request that they sit at his right and left hands in the kingdom of God (Matthew 20:20-28).

[8] Hamas is the radical Islamic party that rules the Gaza Strip.

[9] "Bel el malayeen, bel el malayeen, hanmout men ajl Falessteen."

[10] Bailey and Bailey, *Who Are the Christians?*, 157.

[11] Afif Safieh, quoted in ibid., 162.

12 MARRIAGE AND FAMILY IN ISLAM

[1] "Why Arab Women Still 'Have No Voice,'" *Al Jazeera*, April 21, 2012, www
.aljazeera.com/programmes/talktojazeera/2012/04/201242111373249723
.html.
[2] Polygamy is illegal in Tunisia, but all other Muslim lands permit it, even if
it is not encouraged.
[3] "The things that annul the prayers were set before me: a dog, a donkey and
a woman." *Hadiths of Bukhari*, vol. 1, bk. 9, no. 490 (see also 1.493 and 4.498).
[4] Christine Schirrmacher, *Islam and Society: Sharia Law, Jihad, Women in
Islam*, Global Issues Series (Bonn: Verlag fur Kultur und Wissenschaft,
2008), 4:90.
[5] See sura 4:34.
[6] Hajji means that the man has gone on the Hajj. There is also a Syrian show
with the same theme called *Bab al-Hara*.
[7] There was a well-known case of a man who was jailed because he forgot to
divorce one of his four wives before marrying the fifth.

13 CHRISTIAN–MUSLIM FAMILIES

[1] Muslim men can marry People of the Book (Christians and Jews). However,
a Muslim woman can only marry a Muslim man. So if a Christian man
marries a Muslim woman, their marriage is not legal, and they cannot register their children. When a Muslim man or a Muslim woman becomes a
Christian, they lose the custody of their children, since Christians cannot
father or mother Muslim children.
[2] A child in Egypt is legally the property of his father. Thus if your father is not
an Egyptian, you cannot be either, even if you were born and raised in Egypt.
[3] *Hadiths of Bukhari*, 2658.
[4] *Hadiths of Bukhari*, 29:304, 1052, 1462; and also Sahih Muslim 80:885, 907.
[5] In this way rape becomes a tool of religious and political power, which was
used to such horrific effect during the war in Bosnia and Serbia.

14 EGYPT NOW

[1] This event is referred to as Saad Zaghloul.
[2] Sharif Abdel Kouddous, "What Led to Morsi's Fall—and What Comes
Next?," *Nation*, July 5, 2013, www.thenation.com/article/what-led-morsis
-fall-and-what-comes-next.

[3]Ibid.

[4]Gamal Eid, cited in Haitham El-Tabei, "Concerns over Media Freedoms in Morsi Egypt," *Your Middle East,* January 23, 2013, www.yourmiddleeast .com/news/concerns-over-media-freedoms-in-morsis-egypt_12509.

[5]Morsi was president from June 30, 2012, to July 3, 2013.

[6]Wafaa Sultan, http://m.thevoiceofreason.de/ar/9617#.UykBtYLyoOU .facebook. Author's translation.

[7]Ibid.

[8]In fairness, the Christian West took much of the sixteenth and seventeenth centuries to work out the relationship of church and state. And it continues to have problems around the edges of this issue. But it has largely succeeded.

15 MUSLIM CONVERTS

[1]The principal language of this large Berber group is Kabyle.

[2]This is one reason that convinced me to write this book.

[3]These people cannot publicly say who they are. Since they are proselytizing for Christianity in Muslim lands, their lives are at risk.

[4]"This hadith indicates in two ways that musical instruments and enjoyment of listening to music are *haraam.* The first is the fact that the Prophet (peace and blessings of Allah be upon him) said: "[they] permit," which clearly indicates that the things mentioned, including musical instruments, are haraam according to sharia, but those people will permit them. The second is the fact that musical instruments are mentioned alongside things which are definitely known to be haraam, that is, zinaa and alcohol: if they (musical instruments) were not haraam, why would they be mentioned alongside these things?" Adapted from Muhammad Naasirud-Deen al-Albaani, *al-Silsilah al-Saheehah,* 1.140-41.

[5]For background information on this issue see "Breastfeeding Fatwa Causes Stir," BBC News, May 22, 2007, http://news.bbc.co.uk/2/hi/middle _east/6681511.stm; and Sreeja Vn, "Fatwa on Woman Breastfeeding Man Stirs Debate in Islamic World," *International Business Times,* April 14, 2012, www.ibtimes.com/fatwa-woman-breastfeeding-man-stirs-debate-islamic -world-437360.

[6]"Saudi Clerics Advocate Adult BreastFeeding Adult Men," *Care2,* June 16, 2010, www.care2.com/causes/saudia-arabia-creates-bizzare-breastfeeding -loophole.html. One protagonist was Sheikh al-Obeikan, an adviser to the

royal court of Saudi Arabia. Another who permitted use of a breast pump was Abi Ishaq Al Humaini.

[7] For this reason I cannot reveal my full Arabic name in this book.

16 CURRENT MINISTRY

[1] "Nothing of our revelation (even a single verse) do we abrogate or cause to be forgotten, but we bring (in place) one better or the like thereof. Knowest thou not that Allah is Able to do all things?" (sura 2:106, Pickthall translation).

EPILOGUE

[1] Muslims typically refer to Muhammad as the "Seal" of the prophets—that is, the one who seals off the series.